BREAKFAST with GERANIUMS

and other poems

Mary Waegner

Illustrations
Lyndall von Dewitz

Edited and Published
d'Arblays Press

Also by Mary Waegner
Platform Four at Berkhamsted Station - 2005

This edition first published in 2010 by

d'ARBLAYS PRESS
23 Brookbank Close
Cheltenham GL50 3NL
Gloucestershire

Printed in England by
Creeds - Printers by Design
Broadoak
Bridport, Dorset DT6 5NL

All rights reserved

Copyright © in the individual contributions remains with the authors.

This book is sold subject to the condition that it shall not, by way of trade or otherwise, be lent, resold, hired out or otherwise circulated without the publisher's prior consent, nor in any form of binding or cover other than that in which it is published and with a similar condition including this condition being imposed on the subsequent purchaser.

ISBN: 978-0-9548646-6-8

A CIP record for this book is available from the British Library

To
STEFFI, ROLAND *and* JANI

Contents

	Page
First Breakfast in Marrakesh	9
Setting off in Starlight	10
Waking at Frensham Heights	11
First Day of the Holiday	13
The Silver Park	14
Early Arrival	15
On Waking at Villa Waldheim	16
Chilling Out	17
Breakfast with Geraniums	19
Harald	20
Spring Day at Brantwood	21
The Park in May	22
The Fourteenth of March	24
Bamberg Cathedral	25
Elevenses with Geraniums	26
The River Doon in Spring	27
A Perfect Day	28
May	29
Roses in Graz	31
The Frauenkirche, Dresden	32
Marrakesh at Midday	33
Fulda Cathedral	34
Pedalling to Paradise	36
No Need for Art	37
Trailing our Pasts	38
Hydrangeas	39
Veitsbronn Church	41
Travemünde Revisited	42

Contents

	Page
Meeting in Lyon	43
Contrasts	45
A Walk in the Woods	46
Son, aged 32	47
Requiem for Squeaky	49
The Garden of Meditation at Benediktbeuern	50
Solidades (Loneliness)	51
A Roman Child	52
Jackie	53
Les Tartes aux Fraises	54
Creativity	56
On the Night of my First Birthday	57
Madonnas in Graz	59
Spiekeroog Pheasants	60
Indian Head Massage	61
In Bach's Garden	62
Reappraisal of my Father	63
The Little Donkey	64
Valencia	65
Fürth Windows	66-67
The Visitors	68
En Route to Aurel	69
Farewell to Summer	70
The Waterfall	72
To Wordsworth	75
Choir Practice for "Miracles"	76
Millstätter See	77
Disappointment in Ulm	78

Contents

	Page
Coniston Water	79
Glastonbury Abbey	80
Evening of Song	82
Piazzolla in a Franciscan Monastery	83
The Harpy Eagle	85
The Evening Primrose	86
Sitting in front of a Fire in Grasmere	87
Along the Pilgrim Path	88
Commemoration of Life	90
Death and the Maiden	91
Frost and Sculpture	93
Serenade in the Courtyard behind the Michaelskirche	94
Leaving the Hospital	95
Wintry Bamberg	96
On Hearing Turina's 2nd Piano Trio	98
The Spider	99
Riad Si Said, Marrakesh	100
December Day in Murnau	102
On Leaving the Lakes	103
Bagpipes in Bethlehem	104
Leaving Valencia	105
December Swans	106
The Mount of Olives	108
The Silver Canteen	109
Concert in Millstatt	110
Ode to the River Mur	111

The Poems
An Approach to Poetry

The title of this volume is not alone in its celebration of the beginning of a new day: whether it is Fürth in Germany, Millstatt in Austria, Marrakesh in Morocco or Frensham in England, the pleasurable anticipation of what lies in wait is omnipresent.

In a wider sense, the excitement of exploring a new town, of stepping inside an unknown church, or of attending a concert is very similar to this early morning curiosity. The world abounds in hidden treasures, and the majority of these poems express the author's intense delight in discovering them, not only in Germany, but also further afield.

The poems have been arranged in such a way that they not only follow the course of the sun from dawn to dusk, guiding the reader through the day's cycle, but also reflect the four seasons of the year, moving gradually from spring towards winter.

MARY WAEGNER
Autumn 2010

First Breakfast in Marrakesh

Breakfast was served
With soft-footed courtesy
On a sun-soaked roof.
Seated amidst vast pots
Of palm and oleander,
We basked in the unaccustomed warmth,
Relished the bubbly warble
Of an unknown bird
And savoured the sweetness
Of fresh oranges and figs.
Beneath us throbbed the city,
Harbouring its countless treasures
And its maze of mysteries.
The day stretched temptingly before us:
Magical Marrakesh beckoned.

Marrakesh
October 28th 2008

Setting off in Starlight

I set off in the starlight,
Whipped by a winter wind;
The semi-silence of the city,
Comatose,
Is shattered only
By the random rattle of a shutter.
Pinpricks of lamplight
Reflect the speckled sky,
Where streaks of light
Now shift the weight of darkness.
The underground embraces
Early workers
Into its warren warmth.
I, too, descend, but slowly,
Reluctant to relinquish
The dramatic dawning
Of another winter's day.

Fürth
January 15th 2007

Waking at Frensham Heights

On that first morning
I awoke at dawn,
Flung wide the window
To admit the sounds of Surrey:
Wood pigeons
Were cooing in the copse
While blackbirds cast their song
Upon the fragrant air.
I sensed the playing fields
Beyond the oaks
Would be alive
With rabbit, fox and squirrel.
Hours of music
Waited in an unfurled state:
A prospect of pure pleasure.
Only the drowsy droning
Of a distant plane
Reminded one
Of worlds beyond this haven
In the heart of rural England,
Worlds where the certainties
Of yesterday
Lay now in fragments
On the dusty pavements.

Frensham Heights
July 23rd 2005 (written a few weeks after the terror attack in London)

First Day of the Holiday

No gentle rays of sun
Caress the sheet,
No distant languid waves
Now kiss the sand,
No blackbirds warble airs
On peartree branch.
Instead
The moan and sigh
Of northern winds
Lashing the windows
With sharp darts of rain,
Roaring in intermittent gusts
Of unleashed rage,
Churning the darkened sea
To furious foam.
I wake at dawn
Hugging my happiness
With all the thrill
Of childhood still undimmed.
I cannot wait
To don my anorak and boots,
To brave the elements
And trudge through sodden sand,
Gasping in greedy gulps
The salted air,
Feeling the tingling sting
Upon my skin,
And watching oceans
Heaving to the sky.

Spiekeroog, October 8th 1998

The Silver Park

A silver sheen
Had settled gently
On the meadows overnight;
Each tiny hoar-frost twig
Glistened with whiteness
In the incandescent light.
Beyond the steaming river,
Swathed in soft folds of mist,
The town of Fürth
Rose up, ethereal:
A dreamlike city
Floating on a cloud.
Then suddenly
A shaft of fragile sunlight
Captured the tiny cross
Upon St Michael's spire
And made it flash in all its golden glory:
A new day had begun.

Fürth
February 20th 2007

Early Arrival

Out of the blackness
Of the airport tunnel
The train, bearing its freight
Of plane-dazed passengers,
Was catapulted
Into the frosted Essex fields.
Ducks rose in perfect symmetry
Above the gently steaming lake;
A rising sun vied with a crescent moon
In a sky of pink-tinged promise,
And as the train slid slowly
Into the gloomy guts of
Liverpool Street Station,
My drowsy spirits lifted
In a sudden flash of joy:
I had come home.

London
October 25th 2008

On Waking at Villa Waldheim

I slipped from drowsiness
Into a dream-filled sleep,
Lulled by the chant of crickets.
At dawn, awakened
By a symphony of birdsong,
I gradually remembered
Where I was,
And felt contentment,
Wave upon wave,
Wash through me
Like the cleansing stream
That gurgles to the lake.

Millstatt
May 20th 2007

Chilling Out

Wondering, on waking,
What to do today;
Drowsily toying with options,
Luxuriating in the very act.
Knowing, at breakfast
(Which magically appears),
That by the lake
Speedwells peep shyly
From the grass,
And unseen cuckoos
Call from wooded slopes;
Inviting paths meander
Through multi-coloured meadows,
A Benedictine monastery
Nestles contentedly
In verdant vale.

Books beckon,
A virgin notebook tempts,
My eager bike
Yearns to explore new ground.
This wealth of choices,
All of them mine alone,
Gives me a heady sense
of freedom:
For one brief week
I shed responsibility,
Cast caution to the winds,
And wallow in
My egocentric life!

Froschhausen
May 18th 2009

Breakfast with Geraniums

The wind had dropped overnight
Leaving the water silver-smooth,
Reflecting dim green forests
That slumbered now
Upon the stirrings of the night.
A Mozart flute concerto and an early sun
Filled the veranda,
Where a table by the window,
Laid for one,
Awaited me.
Geraniums in varying states of growth
Sat quietly beside me,
Enhancing the enchanting view beyond.
I could have gazed forever
At the lovely lake;
Add to this: muesli with fresh strawberries,
Steaming coffee, fresh boiled egg:
Body and soul could ask for
Nothing more.

Millstatt
May 20th 2007

Harald

I breathe your name
Over the fields of snow
Watching the huddled sheep,
While the wind
Tosses the thin grey veil of sleet
And sighs in sympathy.
The virgin snow of today
Stretches luxuriously
Into a future question mark,
Beckoning, enticing in its
Multitude of choices.
Yet in between each plan
There slips an image
Distracting as a letter
Found between books:
White-robed, I see you
Being wheeled towards
A temporary oblivion,
And your fear, so well concealed,
Palpitates through the snow
To where I sit
And watch the huddled sheep.

Fürth
February 17th 2000

Spring Day at Brantwood

The day was like a girl
Poised on the brink of womanhood.
Spring had not reached
The tips of twigs
Nor opened rhododendron yet;
The larks sang softly still,
Not yet the full-blown symphony
Of summer's song,
And only snowdrops
Graced in modest groups
The hardened earth,
While all around
The parted lips of daffodils
Hinted at future fullness
And of beauty yet to come.

Grasmere
March 1997

The Park in May

There is a bridal quality
About an early morn in May:
Chestnut and rhododendron
Are adorned in white,
The dormant daisies
Deck the tender grass.
Five fluffy goslings, bridesmaid-like,
Process along a dappled path
That beckons to a nave
Of arching green.
The air is filled with fragrance
And a choir of bursting birdsong
With an intermittent bass line
Of a fat and frolicsome frog.

Fürth
May 12th 2008

The Fourteenth of March

Speeding down the autobahn
With nature awakening either side,
I sit cocooned in glorious Bach
And Piazzolla's "Seasons" turned up loud.
Ahead of me I know
The Danube laps its reedy banks,
Basks in the unexpected warmth,
And all around I sense
The subtle stirring
Of Earth's secret underworld.
Then come Vivaldi's soaring strings
To match my ebullient mood;
And, finally, Adagio for Strings
By Albinoni.

Outside, the trees are tinged
With a blur of faintest green;
And now I find my vision, too, is blurred
Not only by the poignant sadness
Of the haunting melody,
But also by the sudden recollection
That on this day,
So many springs ago,
You died.

Neuburg an der Donau
March 14th 2007 (The anniversary of my mother's death)

Bamberg Cathedral

Like figureheads
Your green-capped towers
Aspire towards the sky,
Enticing April sun to fall
On portals of perfection.
Majestically
You seem to sail
The red-roofed seas
Of Bamberg,
Undaunted by
One thousand years of tempests
With brief lulls of tidal calm.
You have survived
The devil's deviousness,
The malice of mankind.
Triumphant still,
You ride the surging swell,
Endowing each small crest
With hope.

Bamberg
April 8th 2008

Elevenses with Geraniums

She'd made her balcony
A little paradise:
Geraniums bloomed
In blazing reds and pinks,
New buds were swelling
In the August sun,
Which seemed to pour down
Blessings
On this hidden haunt.
Coffee and conversation flowed,
Ending with Bach;
And all day long
One vision that she had
Kept lingering in my mind:
God on his throne
And at his feet sits Bach,
Filling the heavens
With his harmonies
For all eternity.

Fürth
August 23rd 2009 (written after coffee on Judith's balcony)

The River Doon in Spring

Tumbling from the hills,
The river Doon
Flows down through Alloway
Beneath the famous bridge
And past Burns' Monument;
Shortly before it merges
With the open sea at Ayr,
A leafy lane runs peacefully
At its side,
Bordered by banks
Of wild and white-flowering garlic
That on an April evening
Exude a heady scent.
Two herons, long-term residents,
Stand immobile
At the water's edge,
And here and there
Beneath the trees,
Brushed now with hazy green,
An early bluebell
Shimmers shyly
On the banks of the Bonnie Doon.

Ayr
April 9th 2009

A Perfect Day

A cuckoo calling,
And a copper beech
Of symmetry superb
Set in the ancient cloisters.
A bobbing butterfly
Accompanying my ride
Between May meadows
Daubed with dandelions
That served as childhood clocks.
A treasure trove of paintings
In a little lakeside town,
Where horses, cats and deer,
Nestling, invite the viewer
To caress them, lovingly.
Reluctant sunshine
Peers through frothy clouds,
Gilding monastic towers
With a light sublime.
And finally
A random concert
In an unknown church,
Where nine choirs
Offer praise and gratitude
For everything we have –
And I do too.

Froschhausen
May 17th 2009

May

May is the modal verb of months.
The lilac blossoms seem to ask
Permission
For their fragrant pinks and purples,
While lilies of the valley
Bend their tiny heads,
Coyly demure:
Dare we, should we, show our charms?
The pastel hues of
Buttercups and sorrel
In the waving meadow grass
Blur to a haze of softness
In the evening sun,
And birches, sprouting
Tiny pale green leaves
Wonder if they could make
A bolder statement
Like the stalwart beech and oak.
But summer is more blatant
In its full-blown declaration:
The subtleties of
Bluebells in the wood
Shyly emerging
From a bed of last year's leaves
Are not for August's verbs.
May is the modal verb of months:
Can we? Shall we? May we?

Written in Ristorante Sale e Pepe, Bayreuth
May 26th 2001

Roses in Graz

Arches of roses
On the hill
Above the town,
Red-tipped
The bursting buds.
Below, within
The Chapel of St John,
The roses tumble
From the Virgin's lap.
And in secluded cloisters
Round the Cross of Christ
The roses gracefully
Incline their heads,
Inviting us
To step into
This lovely place of peace.

Graz
May 15th 2003

The Frauenkirche, Dresden

Its crowning glory
Is a golden cross,
Made by an English craftsman,
Whose father, in the war,
Dropped bombs.
Upon the altar
Stands the Cross of Coventry,
A copy of the one
They fashioned
From the mediaeval nails
Found in the rubble
Of that other bombed cathedral.
Glorious in its resurrected beauty,
Symbol of hope, and, above all,
Indomitable faith,
The church proclaims its message
To the world:
Love, peace,
And reconciliation.

Dresden
August 18th 2009

Marrakesh at Midday

The call to prayer
Resounds across the rooftops
Of this terracotta city,
Satellite dishes gleam
In the midday sun;
The manic pipes and drums
Fall silent, and the snakes recoil;
We too fall silent
As we sip mint tea
And watch a thin stray cat
Scavenge among some weeds.
The chanting voices fade,
The rhythmic pipes and drums
Reclaim the stage.
We move across the pageant of the square,
Half-dazed,
Past orange vendors and the leaping boys,
Past henna artists and the dancing monkeys,
Past glistening dates and figs, and slumbering snakes,
And dive at last into the dark embrace
Of an enchanted world of dreams:
The labyrinthine Souk of Marrakesh.

Marrakesh
October 29th 2008

Fulda Cathedral

Compulsively the eye is drawn
Across the semi-circular expanse
Of patterned paving-stones
Towards the splendid stone façade.
The belfry chimes a welcome
To the spellbound visitor,
Who can but gaze in wonder
At this symmetry sublime.
The gilded crosses on the domes,
Aspiring heavenwards,
Glint in the midday sun.
The beauty of baroque
Exudes a harmony
That satisfies the senses
In a deeply pleasing way;
The visitor now moves
Towards the door,
Filled with anticipation
And the thrill of exploration:
What treasures lie contained
Within this masterpiece
Of architectural design?

Fulda
February 22nd 2007

Pedalling to Paradise

From wooded banks
A cuckoo greets me
With its minor third;
The Main meanders
In big lazy loops,
As if, in lingering,
It, too, would savour
This idyllic corner of its
Course towards the Rhine.
Sunburnt and solitary,
I cycle past the virgin vines,
Chancing upon a medieval town
Whose houses harbour
Vats of chilled dry wine;
Ahead of me
The town of Vollkach lies,
Nestling within the river's curve,
With ancient moat and walls.
The prospect of a salad in the sun,
A glass of Riesling
And a lovely unknown church
Is all I need
To make me think:
This must be close to paradise!

Vollkach
June 13th 2006

No Need for Art

No need for art
On days like this:
Music - bubble of birdsong
Bursting on the air;
Painting – sunshine on poppies
Nodding in the grass;
Sculpture – soft hills of vineyards
Rising from the Main;

And poetry?
Ah, how the half-formed poems
Throng my mind,
Pulsate in every fibre of the soul,
Yearn like the budding grapes
To reach fruition,
Sated with sunlight
On a day like this.

Sommerach
June 13th 2006

Trailing our Pasts

Trailing our pasts
Like vaporous shed of planes,
We sit and sip our wine.
Who is this black-clad cleric,
Silver-haired,
With intellectual mien,
Sniffing with earthly relish
His ensemble of fine fish?
What vagaries of fate
Have led him here today?
What memories accompany
His every step?
How strange it is to contemplate
The cosmos of his knowledge and his life,
Exclusive territory
Behind the parchment brow.
But then he cannot see
My tendrils stretching back,
Spanning the decades
And the cultural convolutions.
Behind my furrowed brow
A very different past and present lurk;
And yet we smile politely
As I rise to leave,
Trailing my past
Like vaporous shed of planes.

Written in the train from Würzburg to Fürth
February 14th 2005

Hydrangeas

The church was awash with them!
Tumbling, hanging, posing, draping,
A profusion of pink, blue, white,
And palest mauve
Adorned in luscious loveliness
The pulpit, lectern, altar, altar rail;
Each Early English window ledge
A sea of pastel blooms!
Even the chipped stone fingers
Of a long-forgotten lady
Clasped girlishly an orb of petalled pink.
A sudden shaft of sunlight
Streamed through the windows of the choir,
Bathing the lace-cap petals
In a heavenly glow.
Staggered by so much beauty
And artistic skill,
The random visitor
Could only stand and gaze
In spellbound wonderment
At such a floral flourish
In this sacred place of peace.

Written in the train from Westbury to Waterloo
September 4th 2007
(after visiting the Hydrangea Show at St Peter's, Stourton)

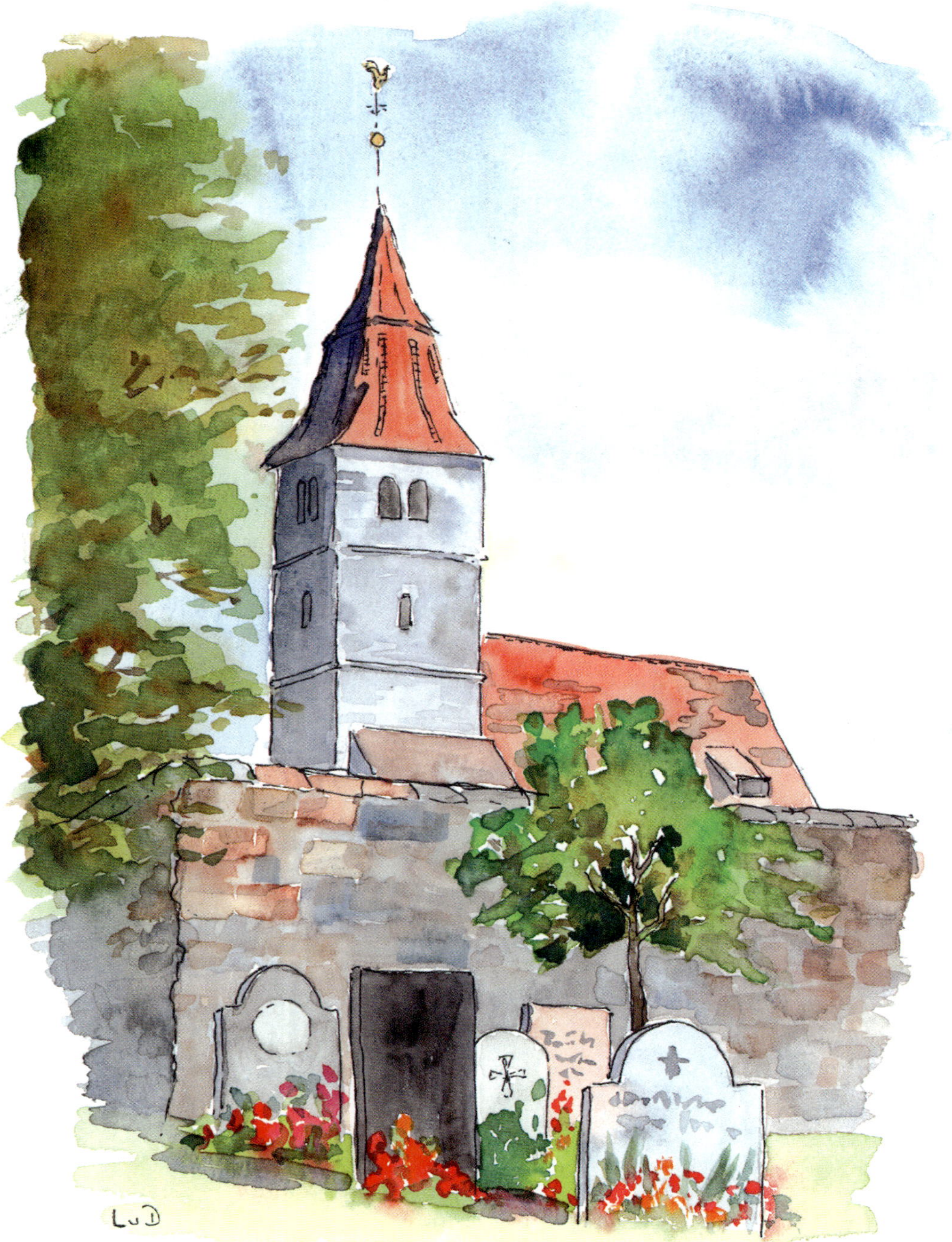
LuD

Veitsbronn Church

Protected by a medieval wall,
The church surveys the land.
Stalwart and sturdy,
It exudes a timeless peacefulness.
White butterflies delight
In luscious blooms
On well-kept graves;
A syncopated song
Bursts from a tiny beak.
Upon the red-tiled steeple
Stands a weathercock,
Immortalised mid-stride;
And from the belfry
Issue forth
The mellow midday chimes
Of ancient bells,
Now, as then.

Veitsbronn
July 18th 2006

Travemünde Revisited

I dodge the jellyfish
Abandoned by the waves;
The sand between my toes
Evokes the memory
Of another me:
A nine-year-old
Who also walked this beach
Dreaming of ballet-dancer fame,
The future one vast blank
Of endlessness.
The hotel where we stayed
Lurks modestly
Behind its new facade
Of dazzling white,
Extending grandly
Over five-star lawns.
Sadness engulfs me
As the seagulls dip;
The taste of salt
And certainty of death
Is rough upon my lips.
My feet have disappeared
Completely now
Beneath the water
And the tug of shifting sand.

Lübeck
August 27th 2003

Meeting in Lyon

Two trains, doing their routine run,
Come snaking down
The two sides of a triangle,
Bearing unwittingly,
Amid their faceless freight,
Two ladies, middle-aged,
In walking boots,
Both smiling quietly to themselves
As they anticipate
The moment of converging
And the chink of Bordeaux glasses.

Written in the train from Karlsruhe to Straßburg
September 21st 2003

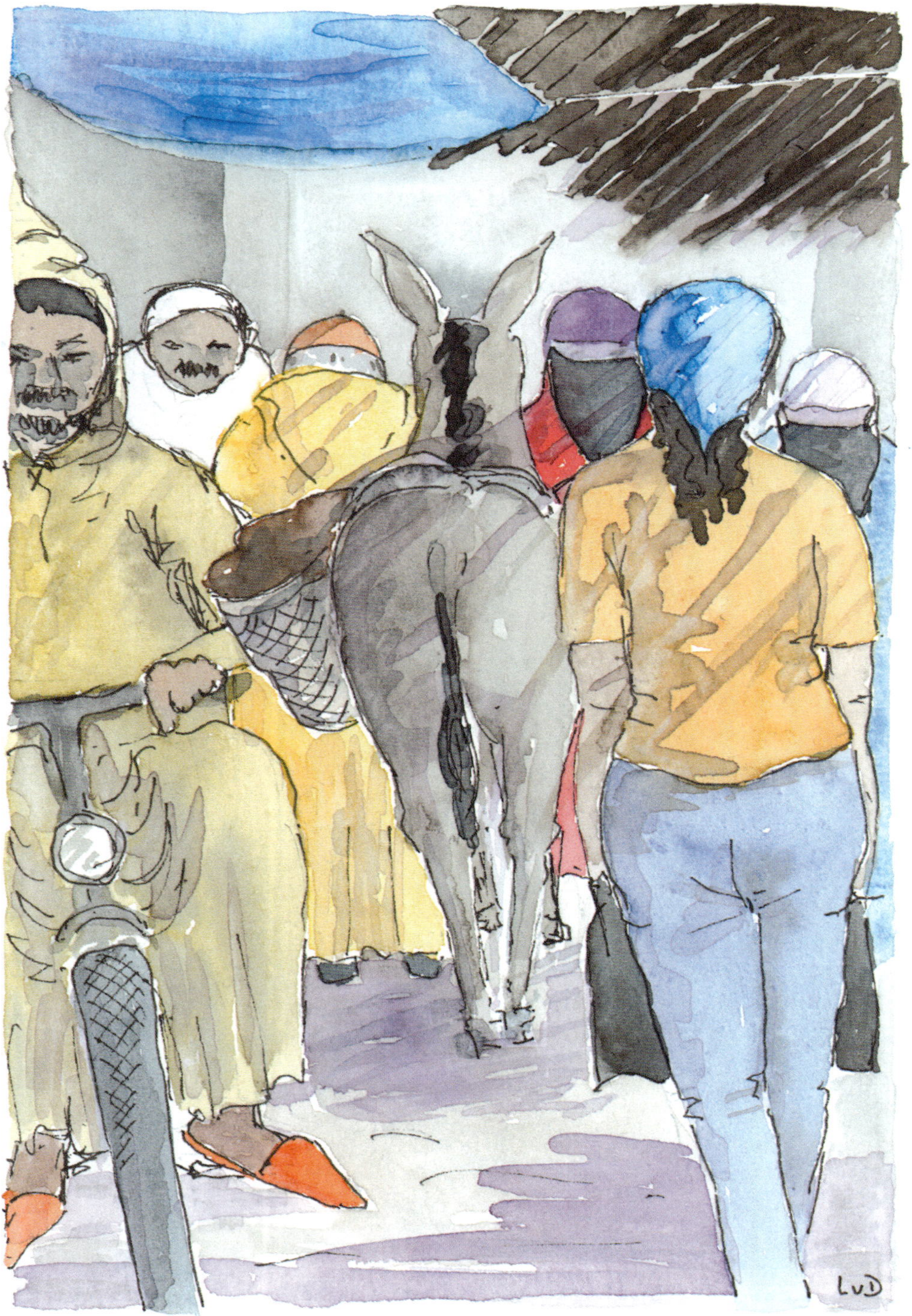
LuD

Contrasts

Step from the colourful chaos
Of the seething streets,
Where mules mingle with scooters
And kaftans jostle with jeans,
Into the cool tranquillity
Of a palace courtyard.
Inhale the heady scent
Of jasmine bloom
And let the choral cadences
Of unseen birds
Among the fragrant foliage
Of pomegranate trees
Caress your senses
As with almond balm.

Marrakesh
October 28th 2008

A Walk in the Woods

Here in these woods I walked
A long, long time ago.
I left the bundle of perfection
We'd produced,
Sleeping a sleep of sated innocence,
And took my wonderment and
Deep, deep joy
Into the Gothic vault
Of naked boughs.
There was no fanfare of acclaim,
No riot of coloured blooms,
Just blackbirds, huddled mutely,
And the crunch of withered leaves.
But never, to me,
Had woodland looked so lovely.

Erlangen
February 24th 2006
(Written in the Glockencafé after a walk in the woods
near the Waldkrankenhaus)

Son, aged 32

Young man with beard
And pack of Gauloises,
Trainers and T-shirt,
Lively, laughing eyes;
Almost protectively
He saunters at my side,
Making me feel diminutive
And old.
I search in vain
To see the fair-haired toddler
In this tall, good-looking man,
But time has intervened.
A memory
Of a small hot hand
Placed trustingly in mine
Stirs like a summer breeze
The surface of my mind.
But that was long ago.
Soon there will be a time
When my hand
Seeks support.

Written in the train from Munich to Fürth
January 18th 2005
(The day after Roland's 32nd birthday)

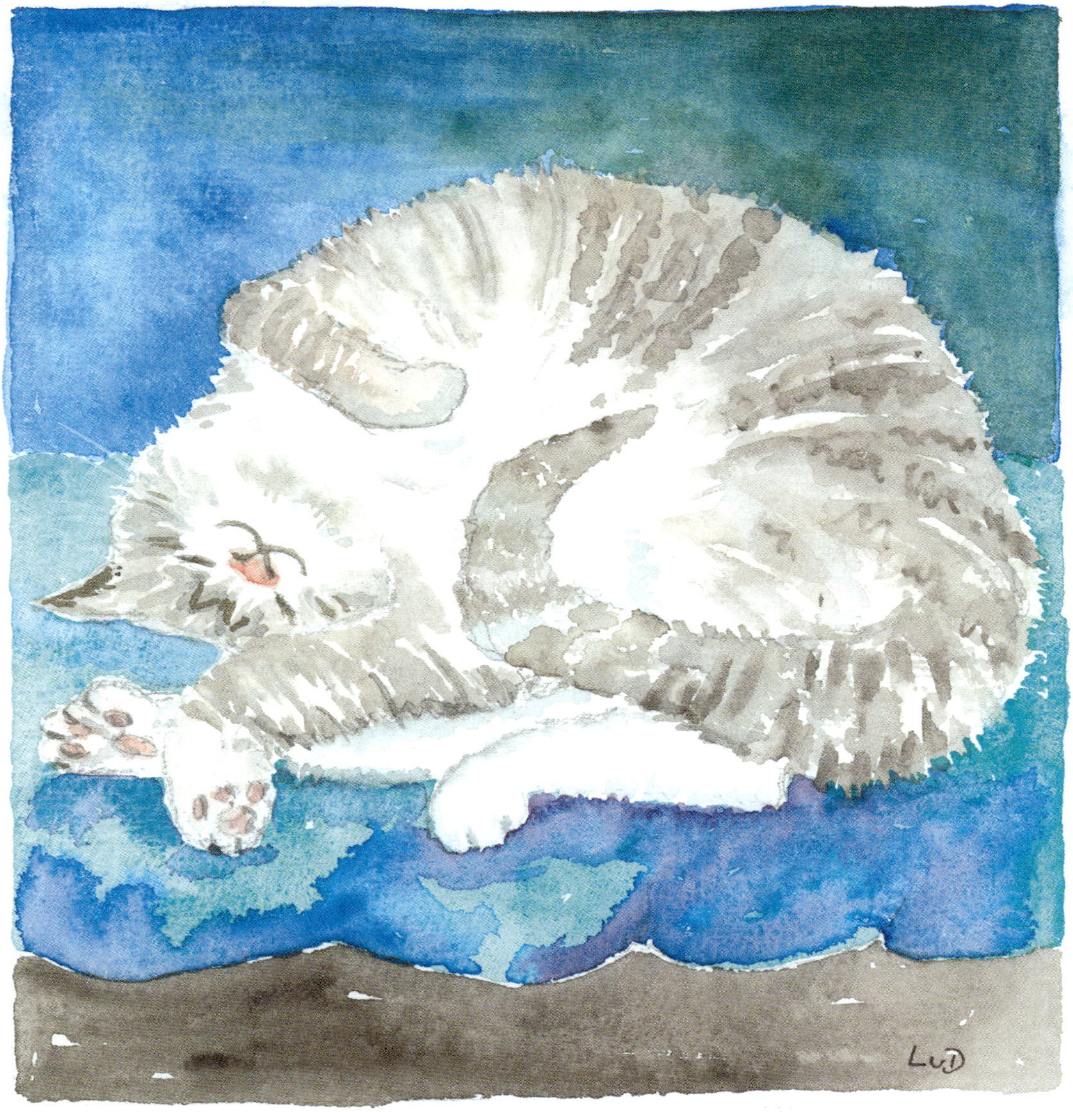
LuD

Requiem for Squeaky

This is the sort of day
When you would
Roll from side to side
In gay abandon
On the dusty path,
Awaiting tummy tickles
On your soft white fur.
Or you would perch
Upon the gatepost in the sun,
Blinking beseechingly
At passers-by
To stroke the small white patch
Beneath your chin.
This is the sort of day
When you would prance
In vain pursuit
Of beetles in the grass,
Or chase a moving twig
With huge black eyes.
And finally you'd flop
On shady balcony
Outstretched full-length
With pointed toes,
Languidly drowsing
In a daze of feline bliss.
This is the sort of day
When you are sorely missed.

Fürth
May 25th 2005

The Garden of Meditation at Benediktbeuern

Set in the shadow
Of the monastery,
A garden of great beauty
And tranquillity
Invites the random guest
To wander through
This labyrinth of life.
We see the centre,
The eternal bubbling spring,
Yet find our footsteps
Steered towards the edge;
Will we in fact achieve
The central point?
We pilgrim the periphery,
Admire the mix of flowers
And healing herbs,
Yearn to discover
Where our centre lies,
Yet, on arrival, wonder:
Is this it?

Froschhausen
May 17th 2009

Solidades (Loneliness)

Fragmented fantasies
Along the pilgrim path
Where memories mingle
With chaotic thoughts.
The sudden burst of ecstasy
As fireworks spark and splinter,
The soul transported
To a lonely sphere
Far, far removed …
Procession of passion and pain:
The women shrieking
And the intermittent
Rhythm of Flamenco,
Threateningly beautiful,
But suddenly disrupted
By the swift sharp arrows
Raining upon the statues in the street,
Spiking collective crowds
With shafts of solitude.
Loneliness lurks,
Waiting to slice
The frail togetherness
Of our existence.
Along the pilgrim path
The footsteps falter.

Fürth
May 25th 2004

(Inspired by a concert in the Marthakirche, Nuremberg with works by the composer Thomas Beimel)

A Roman Child

I wonder if the larks stopped singing
On the day you died?
Or if the clouds released their leaden load
Upon the Lech's green banks?
The bones of roasted pigeon,
Placed beside your coffined corpse,
Exist today, glass-cased,
Upon a plate.
Beside them lie your infant skull
And fragments of your bones.
Your death remains a mystery,
Like your life:
Exhibits number nine and number ten.

Written in the train from Augsburg to Fürth
November 3rd 2004

Jackie

Who is this little boy
With chubby cheeks
And thick dark curls,
Who gazes at the world
With bright, inquiring eyes?
Born on the first of May,
That loveliest of months,
When nature, too, rejoices in new life,
You were the first and only son,
Your parents' pride and joy.
This old, half-timbered house,
Set in the heart of Fürth,
Was where you spent four years;
The cobbled market square,
Scene of familiar sights and smells,
The lovely synagogue
You knew so well,
Your Grandad's shop
Filled with exciting odds and ends,
The lazy Pegnitz
Looping round the town:
This was the little world
In which you played and laughed
And dreamed …

Until that night in June,
Filled with the fragrance
Of the summer trees,
When violent hammering on the door
Shattered your budding boyhood
And stole the light for ever
From your bright, inquiring eyes.

Fürth
April 25th 2009
(Jakob Mandel was shot
in Lemberg Concentration Camp)

Les Tartes aux Fraises

The train chugs slowly
Out of Straßburg
As we bite once more
Into our annual pastry;
Our tastebuds
Swell with sweetness
As the succulence
Of strawberries
Bedded in crispy crust,
Filled with the fragrance
Of long, languid summer days,
Pleasures our palate
With exquisite ruby richness:
We have arrived in France!

Written in the train from Straßburg to Lyon
September 2nd 2006

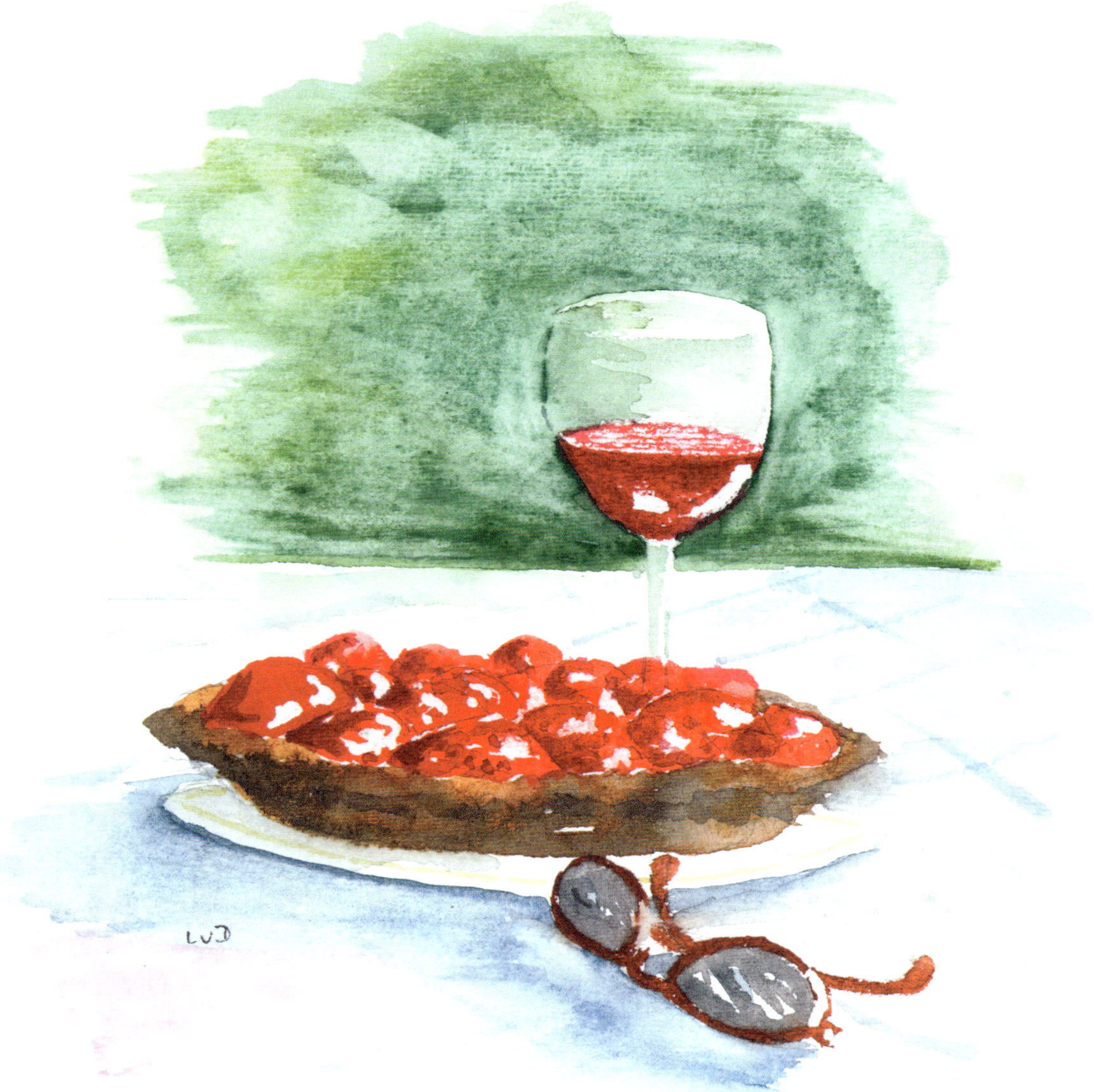
LVD

Creativity

It flows through sculptor's chisel
Into the falling folds of mediaeval wood;
It flows through midnight quills
Scratching by candlelight
A string quartet or song;
It flows through poet's pen
Onto the parchment page,
Through painter's brush
That drips with gleaming oils;
It flows through Gothic stones
Aspiring to the sky,
And also through those hands
That fashion in a country cottage garden
A little paradise on earth.
Since time began
This urge of creativity
Has flowed, unquenchable,
Continuous as the babbling mountain stream
That swells to mighty river,
Filling the world with beauty
And with joy,
And, above all, with hope.

Written in the train from Würzburg to Fürth
January 2nd 2008

On the Night of My First Birthday

Another church destroyed.
The first bombs hailed upon
St Michael's Church in Munich
On the night of my first birthday.
I lay on "hostile territory",
Cradled in innocence
And blissful ignorance
Of war and wickedness,
Death and destruction.
Six decades on,
I sit within the resurrected church,
Musing upon the randomness
Of birth and origin,
The idiocy of man destroying man,
And pray that the peacefulness
Encapsulated here
Within this church
May radiate throughout
Our war-torn world.

Munich
January 18th 2008

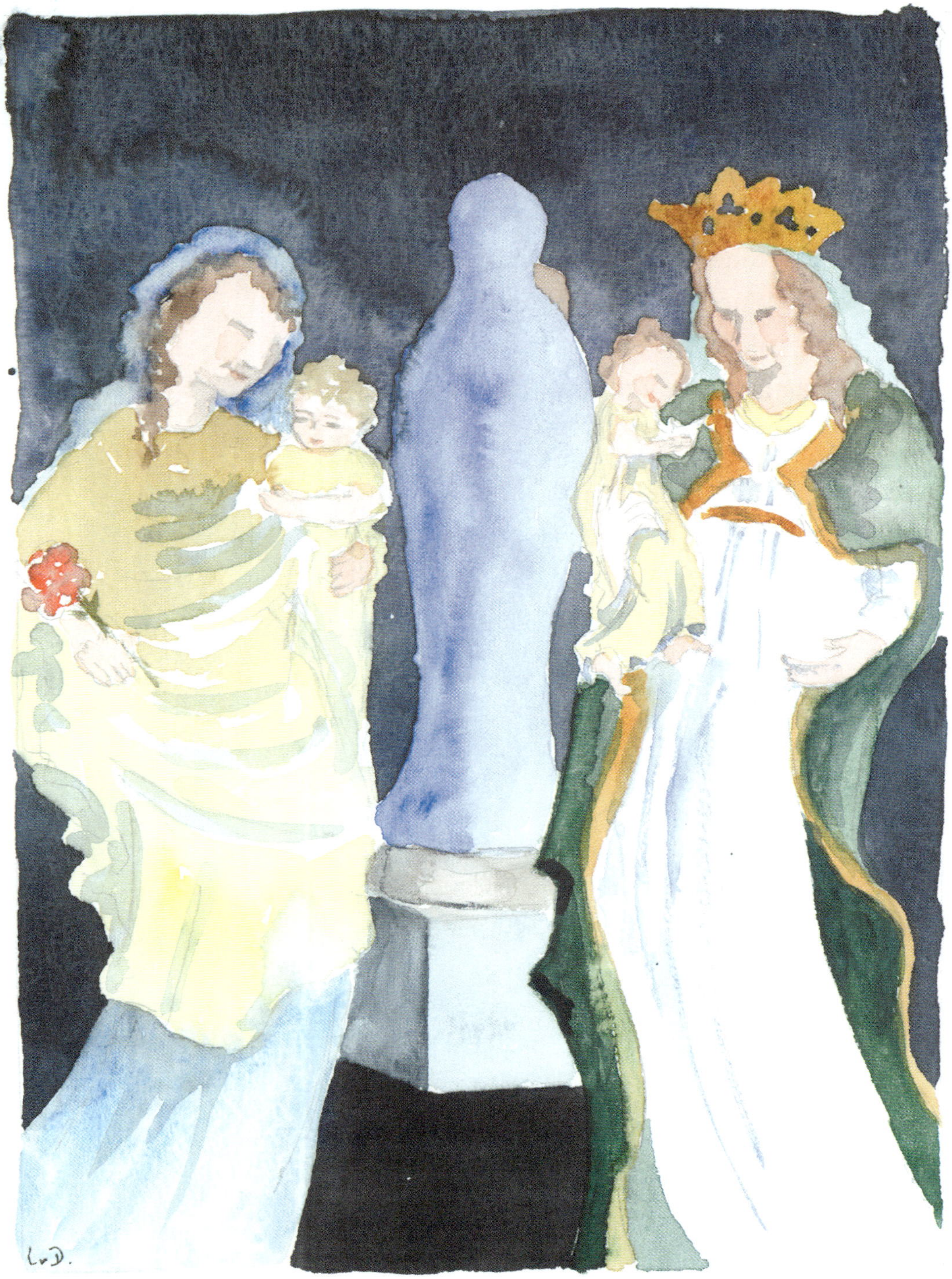

Madonnas in Graz

We step from sunlight
Into a darkened room;
Silence surrounds us
Like a veil of silk.
Madonnas, mediaeval,
Stand immortalised,
Bathed in a light divine,
And spread their mantle
Like a gentle shroud of love.
Their presence dominates
The darkened room.
I pray that their soft mantles
Might encompass
Us as well.

Graz
June 29th 2006
(written after visiting the "Schutzmantel"
Madonnas in the Alte Galerie in Schloß Eggenberg)

Spiekeroog Pheasants

Amid the rosehips and the stunted oaks
Wild pheasants lurk.
They strut, oblivious to humankind,
On dune and dike,
And trail
Their feathered trains
Of phosphorescent silk.
The sated tourist eye
That sees, unseeing,
Butterflies and shells,
Acknowledges perfunctorily
The birds.
But those with time to linger
And to look
See with increasing wonderment
And awe
The artistry of nature
Unsurpassed
In each fine feather´s sheen.

Spiekeroog
October 13th 1998

Indian Head Massage

A dewdrop landed
In the lap of the world,
Poised for an instant
On the cobweb hammock
Strung between blades of grass,
Graceful as a ballerina's tiptoe;
Camellia petals opened
In the walled garden;
An incandescent stag
Leapt in a perfect arch
Into the nothingness of space.
Fragrance of jasmine
On a balmy Spanish night
Suffused the senses,
Already drifting downstream
On a swell of heavenly sound.

Frome
September 4th 2007
(Written after an Indian head massage by Amma)

In Bach's Garden

Capture the butterfly
Alighting on a marigold;
Preserve the subtle scent
Of lavender and rose;
Let swallows linger in the sky,
Midflight;
Imprint upon the eye
The rambling vine.
Above all, hear once more
The lovely sound
Of clavichord and organ
Played in a room
Where once a baby
Toddled into boyhood,
Harbouring unbeknown
Within his being
The slumbering seed of genius
That would one day
Change the world.

Written in the train from Eisenach to Fulda
July 4th 2006
(After a visit to Bach's birthplace in Eisenach)

Reappraisal of my Father

Fragments of thought
Float down the intricate
Meandering of my mind:
Upon the banks
Old driftwood, darkly secret,
Lies in ragged piles;
Whirlpools of half-forgotten rage
And childhood wounds
Churn in unending murkiness.
The sense of liberation
That I first felt on your death,
(The bondage broken
And the fear dissolved)
Has floated to obscurity.
Instead, I sense a bond, though frail,
A constant current
Where small coloured leaves of love
Sail softly to the sea.
My task is now to sift
The filial flotsam on the shore
And carry with me only
Fragments of gratitude and love.

Fürth
May 4th 2008

The Little Donkey

I dream of a little donkey
Waiting with one leg bent
And hoof half-raised
In a pose of
Centuries-old submission.
Stoically he bears
His master's stinging whip,
The sores upon his back,
The overloaded cart.
His undernourished body
Reveals the sharpness of the bones
Beneath the mangy fur;
His eye is dull.
At last the load is fastened:
Roll upon roll of carpet.
Crack goes the whip!
The little donkey
Strains his aching limbs,
Slowly resumes the rhythm
Of his daily toil,
And makes his weary way
Across the crowded square.

Nuremberg
December 8th 2008

Valencia

Beneath sweet-scented pines
And orange trees
They sit or stroll;
Late-blooming roses line their path,
While palm fronds proffer shade.
Ancient and modern bridges
Span this spacious park
Where once the mighty Turia
Wended its seaward way.
Crowning the new-born valley
Three splendid structures –
White mosaic and glass –
Curve in a daring blend
Of symmetry and space.
Beyond the people's park
The pale stone palaces and churches
Drowse in the late November sun.

Valencia
November 11th 2007

Fürth Windows

Their heads emerge
From tortoise-shell security
To sniff the air
And reconnect with life
Beyond the microcosm
Of their stifling cares.

Behind them we can glimpse
The dimness of a room
Proffering protection –
But perhaps imprisonment.
Behind them, too, we vaguely sense
The vast complexity
Of history in their wake:
The personal mosaic
Of the decades
That each individual trails,
A pattern of such intricate design
That our imagination falters.
We hustle by, half-envious,
Perhaps contemptuous, too,
That some should have the time
To gaze and contemplate.
Yet let us not pass judgment:
Who knows the background
Of each Fürth-framed face?
Who knows what richness may be found
In simply being, and not doing,
For a while,
But just partaking peacefully
Of life in all its facets
In the street world down below.

Fürth
February 28th 2007

The Visitors

The basket of birdseed
Did it.
She had hoped for a
Bluetit or two,
A sparrow perhaps.
So their arrival
In a soft flurry
Of feathers
At the drowsy point
Of a Sunday afternoon
Caught her unawares
Planting a wisteria.
Their gentle cooing
On the pale stone wall
Seemed like a
Soothing song of friendship.
They came next day,
And the next,
And every day:
Two turtle doves
With plumes of pinkish white,
Fluttering softly
To the little paradise
She had created,
Bearing, invisible,
A tiny sprig of olive.

Written on the train between Bayreuth and Fürth
May 17th 2000

En Route to Aurel

No-one could know,
Glancing perfunctorily
At them as they
Picnicked at the zoo
Or slumped in slumber
On the Lyon train.
No-one could know
That in their rucksacks
Lay, cocooned in velvet,
Two lovely pipes
Of sleek, smooth wood.
No-one could know
That in five days
Their mellow sound
Would touch the timbers
Of a tiny church in France,
Touch, too, the hearts
Of those who'd gathered there,
As these two travellers,
Clad now in long black skirts,
Breathe life and beauty
Into pipes of wood.

Written in the train from Straßburg to Lyon
September 4th 2004

Farewell to Summer

Tall beech trees
Shed their golden glory
On the woodland path
That snakes invitingly
Into the secret dimness.
Forgotten wisps of cloud
Rise softly from the treetops,
Sending their signal of
Nostalgic evocation.
Children once more,
We shuffle through the leaves,
Inhale forgotten fragrances,
And smile to see
The gallant rosehip
Bobbing on naked branch;
Along the wayside
Clusters of campions
Nod farewell to summer.

Fürth
23rd October 2007

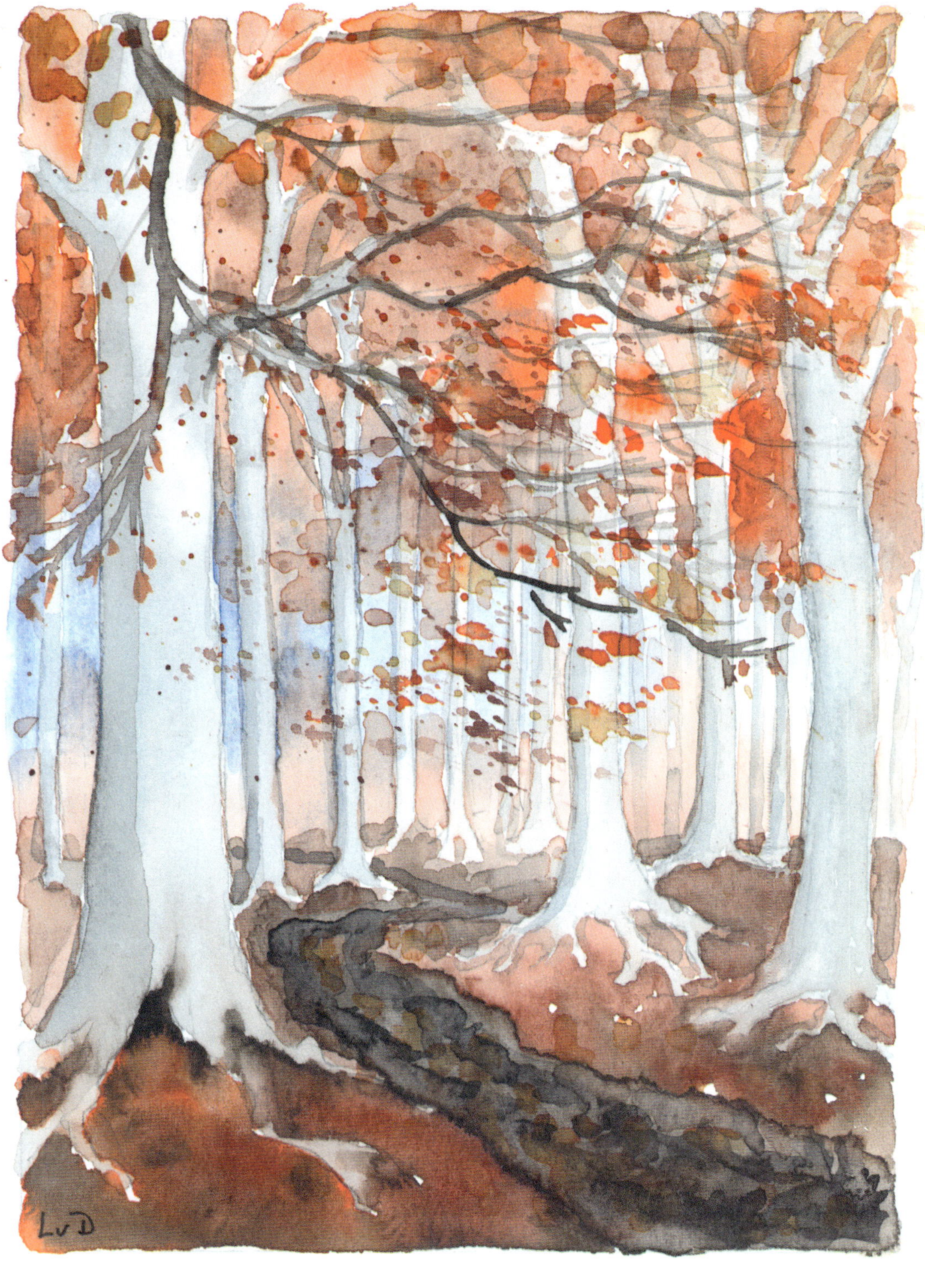
LvD

The Waterfall

Carving its mighty path of foam
The waterfall comes
Crashing, splashing
With a thunderous roar
Over the sleek black rock.
Defiant, carefree,
Like a wayward spirit
That is bound to
No conventions,
Petty laws,
But breathes the air
Of bracken on the fells
And knows
The song of robin
In the rosehips,
It winds its tortuous way
Through deep ravine
And over stones
Worn centuries-smooth,
Until, submissive, gentle,
It meanders
Through the plain:
Only the muffled roar
Of distant water falling
Hints at the unleashed spirit
At its source.

Grasmere
October 13th 1996

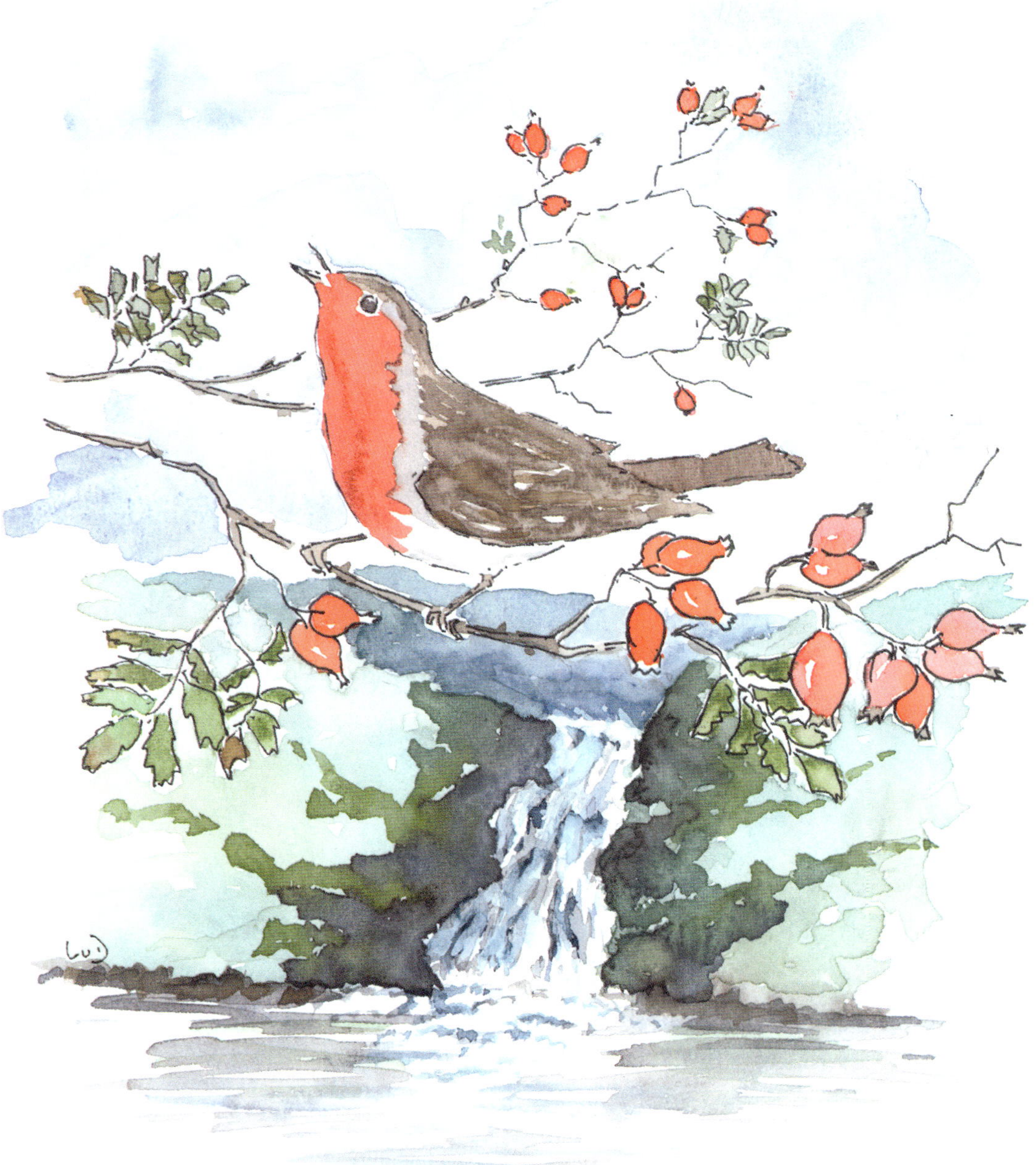

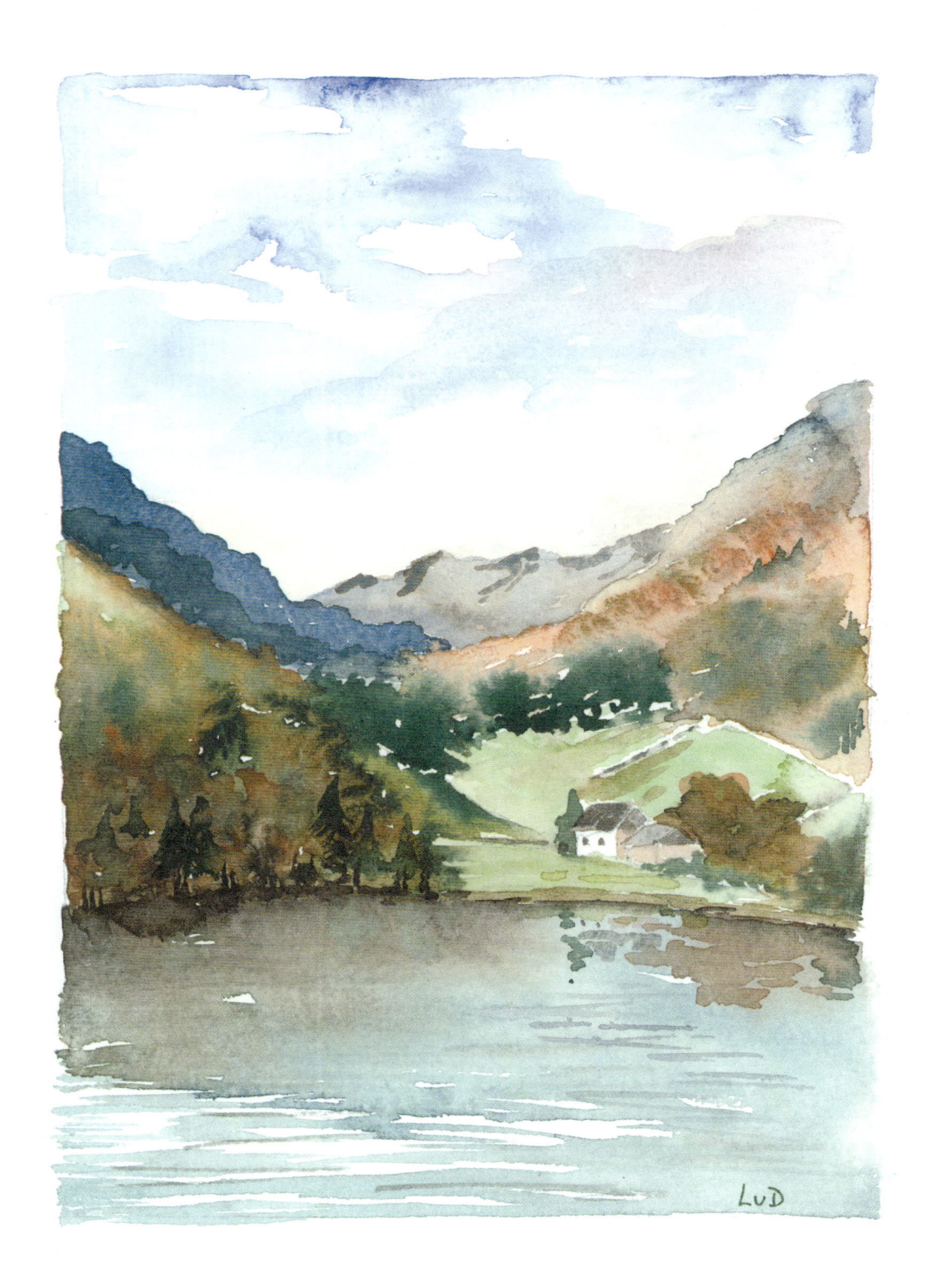
LUD

To Wordsworth

Your feet once walked
Along this well-worn track
Beside the lake,
Felt the soft rustle
Of the sodden leaves,
The crunch of gravel
By the water's edge.
Your eyes once feasted
On these rugged hills,
Dormant, yet vibrant
With a hidden strength;
Gazed on the slaty blue
Of gleaming lake,
Its waters troubled
Only by a diving swan.
Your eyes beheld
The chariots of cloud
Riding relentlessly
Across the fells,
Draping the burnished woods
In silent grey.
You, too, inhaled
The scent of autumn's dampness,
The smell of burning coal
From cottage fire.
You heard the dripping
Of the beech at dusk,
The endless chatter
Of the babbling brook,
The rippling of the waves
Upon the stones.
Humbly I follow in your steps,
Aware of sated senses
And a joyous heart;
Aware, too, of the sheer perfection
And the beauty of your words.

Grasmere
October 11th 1996

Choir Practice for "Miracles"

Autumn lay lurking
In the darkened yard;
Dead leaves
Stirred in the silence.
I watched myself
Creep cautiously
Into the desolation of the dying day,
Conscious of feeling foreign
In this eerie part of town.

But then I heard,
Floating upon the damp dark air,
The heavenly sound
Of song:
The voices rose and fell
Upon the autumn night
In sweetest harmony;
Standing transfixed
Amidst the rotting leaves,
I felt a surge of unexpected joy:
I listened, full of wonder,
To the words
I'd given birth to:
A miracle indeed.

Written in the train from Bamberg to Fürth
October 13th 2005

Millstätter See

Wild roses tumbled to the stream
In wanton disarray;
A cheeky sparrow danced
Towards my plate;
In the slow setting of the Alpine sun
Upon the rippling lake
The world stopped turning for a while
And banished ugliness and
All things evil.
It was a magic span of time,
The sun gilding the plumage
Of the homing swan
And soothing all our yesterdays of discontent.
The breeze had ebbed now,
Wafting away the world of worries
That had travelled in my wake.
The lazy lapping of the darkening waves
Was balm to every sense:
All that disturbed
The beauty of this hour
Was the awareness
Of its transience.

Millstatt
May 19th 2007

Disappointment in Ulm

Beneath that matchless mediaeval spire
The graceless shops
Flaunted their wares
With blatant disrespect.
Hamburgers in glass palaces
And scraggy chickens,
Battery-raised,
Turning relentlessly
In greasy vans.
Functional buildings,
Modern, lacking charm,
Obliterated the cathedral base;
But as I stepped
Into the darkening square
The floodlights hit the tympanum,
Bathing the sculpted figures
In a pool of gold.
Displeasure faded instantly;
I gazed in awe,
Anticipating treasures stored within.
But that interior I found withheld,
The portals bolted:
I had come too late.
Sadly I turned,
Engulfed once more
By greed and garishness,
Unholy outcrop of our age.

Fürth
November 18th 1992

Coniston Water

At dusk
The heavy curtain
Of the clouds
Was slowly raised,
Revealing
Wooded hills
Bathed in a pale gold light.
The lake, too,
Caught the image,
Danced with a thousand stars
To match the smouldering glow
Of beech and birch.
And down a distant gully
From great height
A thin white streak
Of waterfall
Cascaded to the lake.
A balustrade of fir trees
Lined the ridge
Between the hills,
And just below the curtain
Of the cloud
Six tiny windmills did their dance
Of flailing arms,
While, far below,
The lake exhaled
Thin puffs of evening mist.

Grasmere
October 12th 1996

Glastonbury Abbey

I sat upon the ancient Isle of Avalon,
Watching the subtle stirring of the fish
Beneath a lid of waterlilies,
Whose rose-cream petals slept on beds of green.
The sad stark ruins of the Benedictine abbey
Soared in memorial grandeur
Over sweeping lawns;
Nature, indomitable, had sprouted tiny tufts
From crevices in long-neglected stones,
Where formerly soft furls of incense
And dark candle smoke
Had left their lingering fragrance.
A gentle breeze of wistfulness
Stirred in the cider orchard
By the pond:
A damsel-fly hovered
In iridescent splendour
Above the thistled grass;
No sound except the timeless plop of fish
And croak of frog;
A sacred site indeed
This Isle of Avalon.

Glastonbury Abbey
September 3rd 2007

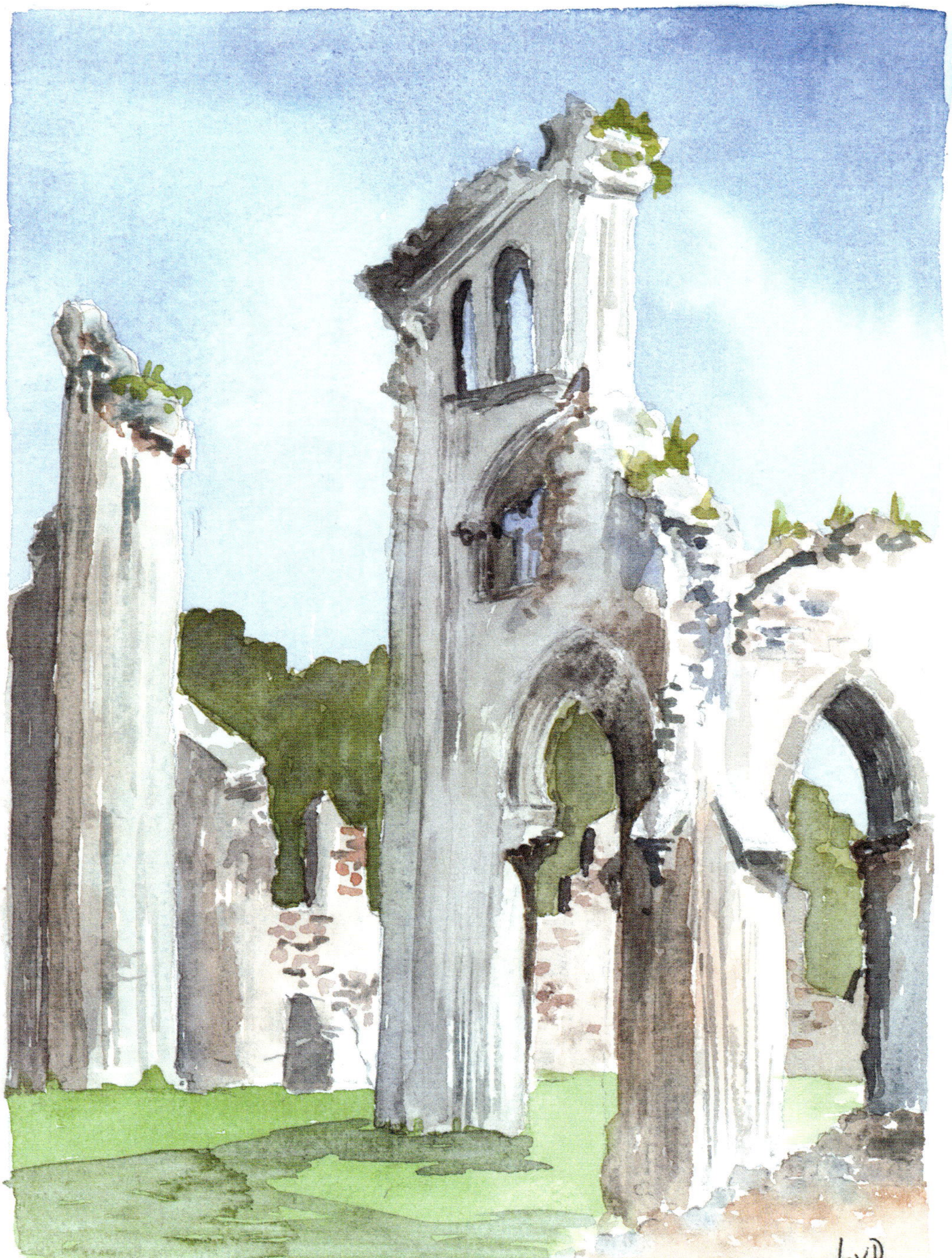
LvD

Evening of Song

Outside the roads are gleaming,
Steaming from the rain:
Within, a touch of
Sixteenth-century Florence.
The singers enter
Through the mirrored doors,
And then their beautiful young voices,
Throbbing with all their hopes and aspirations,
Transport us to that place
Where music mingles
With such pearls of poetry
That the soul is stirred
Beyond belief,
Sated with sweetness
Like a bee
That chances on a rose garden
In June.

Written in the train from Graz to Linz
June 30th 2006
(After a concert of arias and songs
by music students in the Florentiner Saal, Graz)

Piazzolla in a Franciscan Monastery

Here in this ancient church
Where once Franciscan monks
Stepped sleep-dazed
From their cells
To pray at dawn,
The throb of tango rhythms
Issues from dingy doors
In backstreet Buenos Aires,
Stabbing the starlight
Of a sultry summer night.
The Gothic vaults,
Soaked in the plainsong
Of another age,
Span with an easy grace
Eight hundred years.

The past and present merge,
The future too,
Contained within our random
Thoughts
and dreams
That weave their tangled threads
Between the syncopated notes.
The strings subside in sadness,
But the music lingers
In the silence
Of the stones
And in the very substance
Of our souls.

Fürth
August 13th 2005
(Written after a concert of
The Academy of St Martin in the Fields
in Saalfeld:
The Four Seasons of Buenos Aires
by Piazzolla)

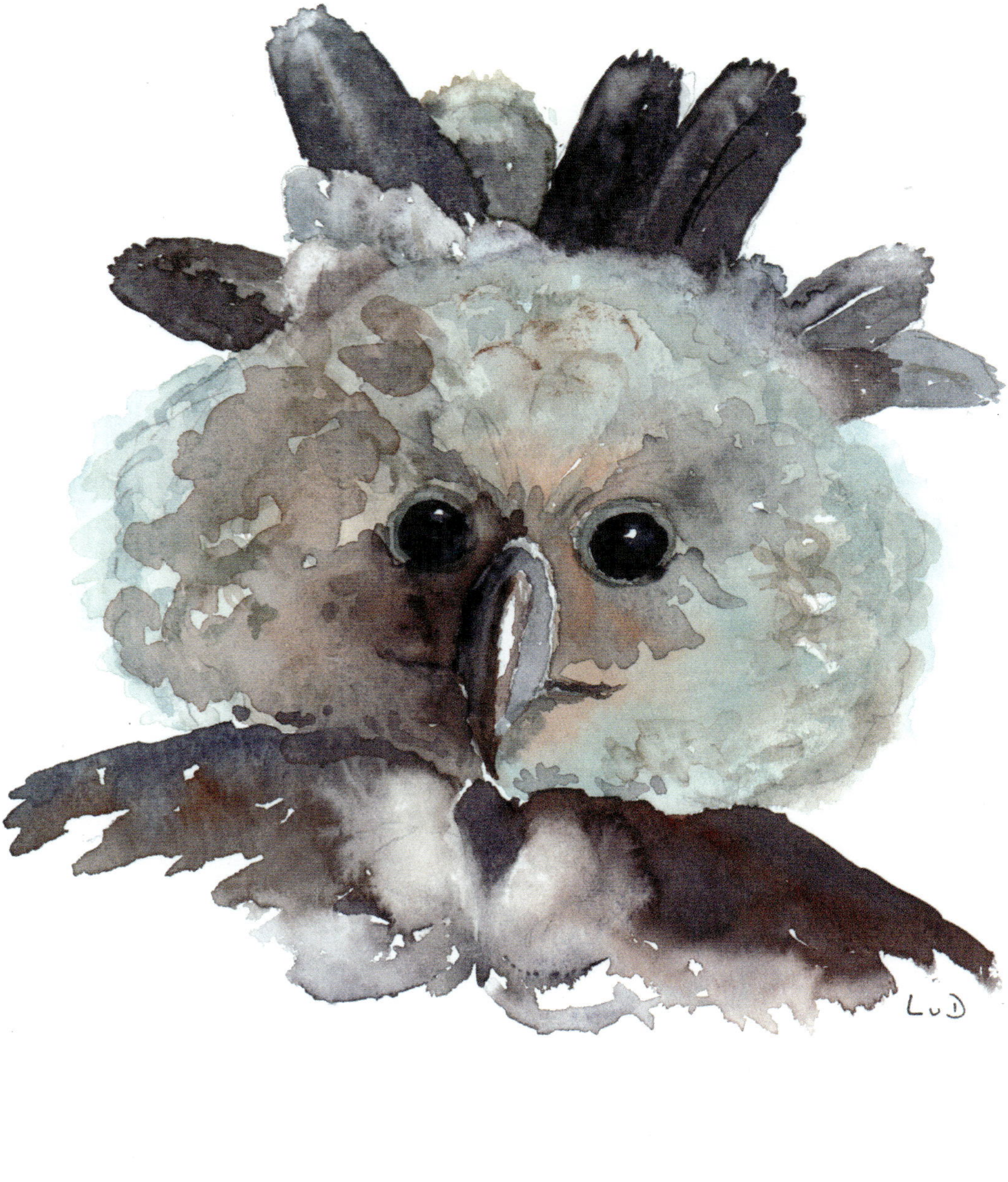
LuD

The Harpy Eagle

He sits immobile on his branch,
Regards the dripping dampness
With an eagle eye.
Draped like an academic gown,
The vast black wings
Fold on his snow-white shirt.
The professorial air
And grim ferocious mien
Are somewhat mitigated
By a row of feathered curls
Cresting his crown.
But most endearing
Is the intermittent sound
That issues from his beak:
No raucous squawk of anger
But a sweet and gentle chirp.

Fürth
October 4th 2007

The Evening Primrose

We wait.
The light is fading fast,
The air grows moist.
With bated breath
We gaze upon
The bulging bud,
Willing it
To divulge its secret self.
A tiny tremor
As the lower petal
Seems to breathe
Then gently swell;
And now the others tremble too,
As slowly, slowly,
They unfurl themselves
In glorious slow-motion
Until the newborn yellow bloom,
A full-blown evening primrose,
Sheds its radiance on the dusk
And on our little spellbound group.

Written in the train from Straßburg to Lyon
September 4th 2004
(after an evening in Peter and Sarah's garden)

Sitting in front of a Fire in Grasmere

I warmed my hands
At the flames of the past,
Watched them consume
The vanished decades
In a crackling dance of death.
My eyes rested again on
Fireguard, scuttle, tongs,
Those props of childhood winters,
And I mourned the death
Of those who'd peopled
All those hearth-side years,
Whose own hearth now was cold.
And the leaping flames,
Licking the coal with darting tongue,
Threw a patterned light
On my thawing hands,
Then, as now.

Grasmere
March 1997

Along the Pilgrim Path
(Nuremberg to Roßtal)

Herb robert my companion
On the pilgrim path,
And here and there
A foxglove in the woods.
I thought of all those pilgrims
Who had trod this path before,
Without the luxury
Of sturdy boots
And suncream and a map.
The endless miles before them
Stretched in a chain
Of penance and of pain
Over the hills and forests
Of four European lands.
Yet through all hardship:
Sickness, heat and damp,
The bleeding blisters
And rheumatic aches,
They trudged unswervingly
Towards their goal,
The image of St James's
holy shrine
Upholding them
And strengthening each step.
Death lay in wait for some;
The howl of lonely wolves
Resounded through the blackness
Of the woods.

My feet were sore
When I returned by train
To soothing bath and bed.
For me, a lovely walk
Through dappled glades
With glimpse of startled deer.
Mine was no pilgrimage like theirs;
And I was humbled
At the thought
Of all those pilgrims of the past
Wending their weary way
Along the path to Spain.

Written in the train to Darmstadt
June 28th 2004

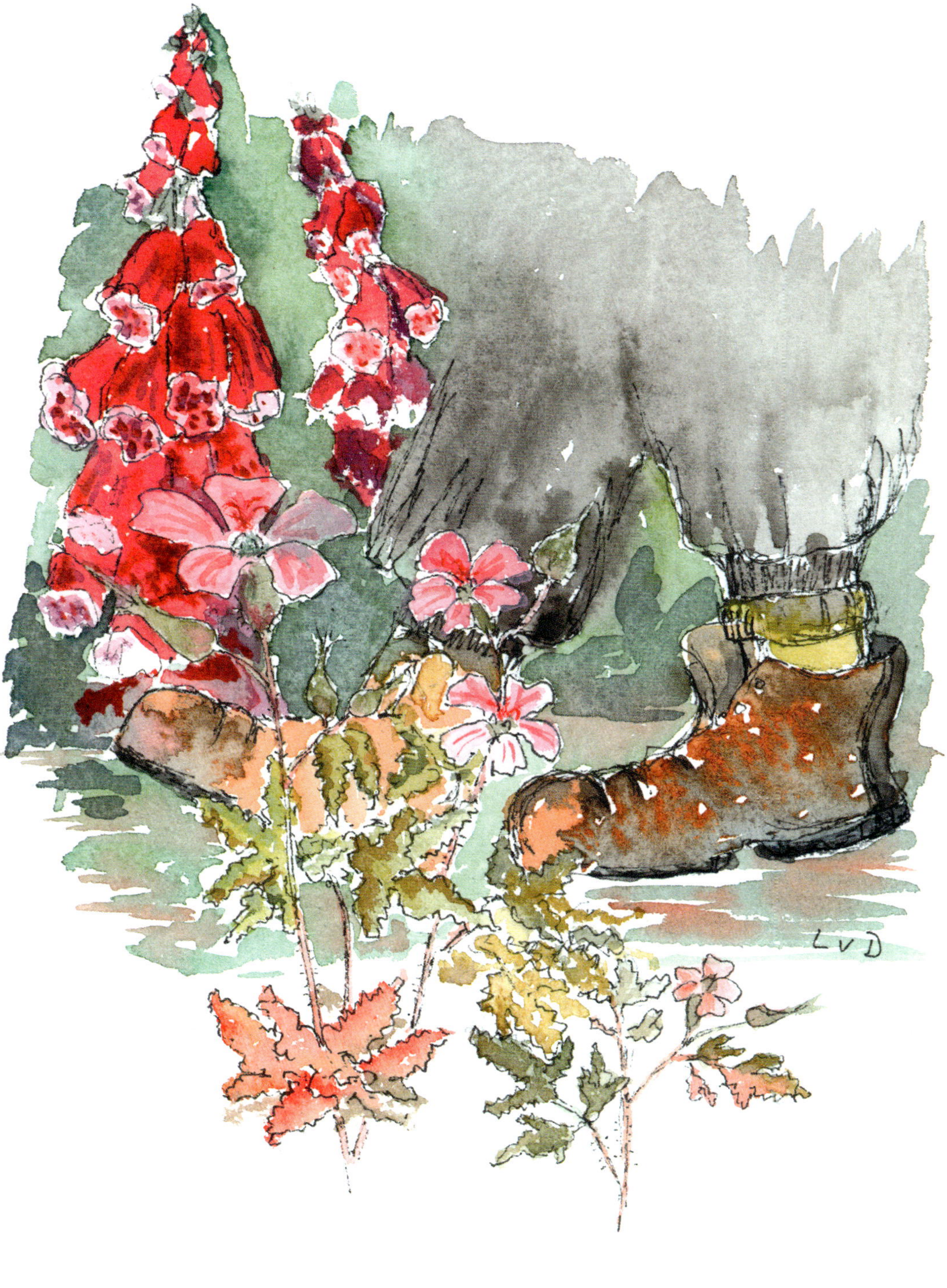
LVD

Commemoration of Life

Striding across the bridge
That spans the Main,
Watching the murky swell
That swirls below,
I sense a sudden surge of
Existential joy;
The frozen vineyards dark beyond the fortress,
The clouds foretelling snow,
The town a silhouette of soaring spires
And splendid palace domes,
All so familiar, yet delightfully foreign still,
And I inhale in greedy gulps
The richness of the world.

Written in the train from Würzburg to Fürth
February 14th 2005

Death and the Maiden

The aching sadness
Of the opening theme
Envelops us.
We see the tiny coffin
Bravely borne on high
By bearers, stony-faced with grief.
Now it is lowered,
Gently, tenderly,
Into the waiting earth;
Flowers fall from fingers
That so recently
Had clasped her frightened hand
And stroked her soft pale cheek.
Then comes
An all-consuming anger,
A violent fury
At the waywardness of fate.

Harshly the bows
Now strike the strings
In strident chords of rage.
But listen now:
The violin soars to heights
Of softest sweetness,
Fluttering on the air
Above the haunting melody below;
Is this perhaps her soul,
So beautiful and pure,
That flies in joyous liberation
Up, up to the skies,
Just like the butterfly
She'll never see again?

*Written in the train from Vienna to Munich,
April 22nd 2009
(After hearing a performance of
Schubert's String Quartet D810
"Der Tod und das Mädchen"
played by The Carcassonne String Quartet)*

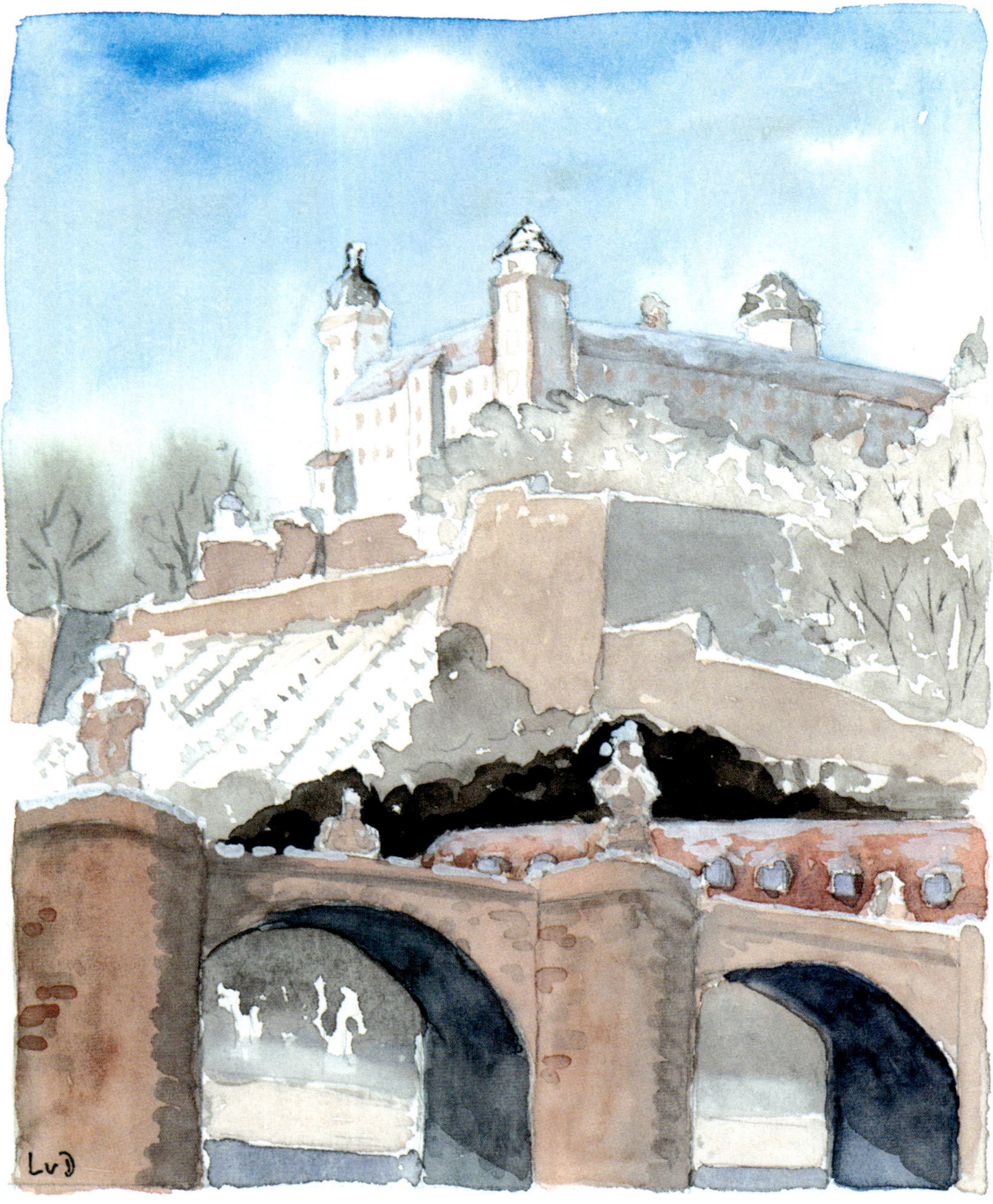
LvD

Frost and Sculpture

Dreamlike the fortress on its whitened hill,
The sparrows silenced by the frosty chill;
The landscape, silver-sprayed, appeared unreal,
Shrouded by winter's sharp-edged icy seal.

Inside, a host of beauteous figures stood,
Carved by a genius hand from chunks of wood:
Elegant finger, rippling, pulsing vein,
A mouth expressing ecstasy or pain.

A gently dimpled chin, a graceful pose,
An oval face more lovely than a rose;
The folds, so tangible, of sumptuous gown,
The suffering eyes beneath the thorny crown.

These were no lifeless works of sculpted art:
One sensed the spirit and the throbbing heart.
In contrast, quite unreal the outside world,
Where frost on every twig and blade lay curled.

Written in the train from Würzburg to Fürth
February 2nd 2006
(after a visit to the Riemenschneider room in the
Marienberg Museum, Würzburg)

Serenade in the Courtyard behind the Michaelskirche

The swallows swooped,
Missing miraculously
The barn roof and the spire,
Sensing the summer shower
Encapsulated still
Within the darkening cloud.
A sparrow on an aerial
Added his feeble chirp
To clarinets and voices
In the mediaeval yard
Behind the church.
Lime-trees exhaled their sweetness
On the evening air;

Petunias tumbled
From a nearby balcony
In colourful cascades.
Into a sultry sky
The Mozart arias soared,
Mingling melodiously
With church clock chimes,
Earthly reminder
On this rapturous night
That time had not,
As it had seemed,
Stood still.

Written in the train to Darmstadt
June 28th 2004

Leaving the Hospital

Half-guilty to be free
While you are not,
Greeting the world
Of buses revving at the gate
And pigeons
Vying for a place on church's tower,
I step half-dazed
Into my life again.
All day, and yesterday,
I sat in sad communion
In your room,
Watching you struggle
In your jail of hell.
The walls submerged us,
And the clocks stood still.

The evening air is chill,
But crisp and sweet.
The snow starts falling
As the train departs.

*Written in the train
between Bayreuth and Fürth
February 20th 2000*

Wintry Bamberg

The Zweigelt wine
Spreads languor through my veins,
The embryo of a poem
Stirs;
I sit here in this mediaeval mill
And relish Advent candles
And roast goose.
Outside, the dripping eaves
And sleety wind
Proffer no welcome
To the random guest;
Only the knowledge
Of that loveliest of buildings,
Bamberg Cathedral,
On its crowning hill,
Make the long foot-wet walk
Up over icy cobbles
To the spacious square
A hundredfold worthwhile.

Written in the Brüdermühle restaurant, Bamberg
28th November 2005

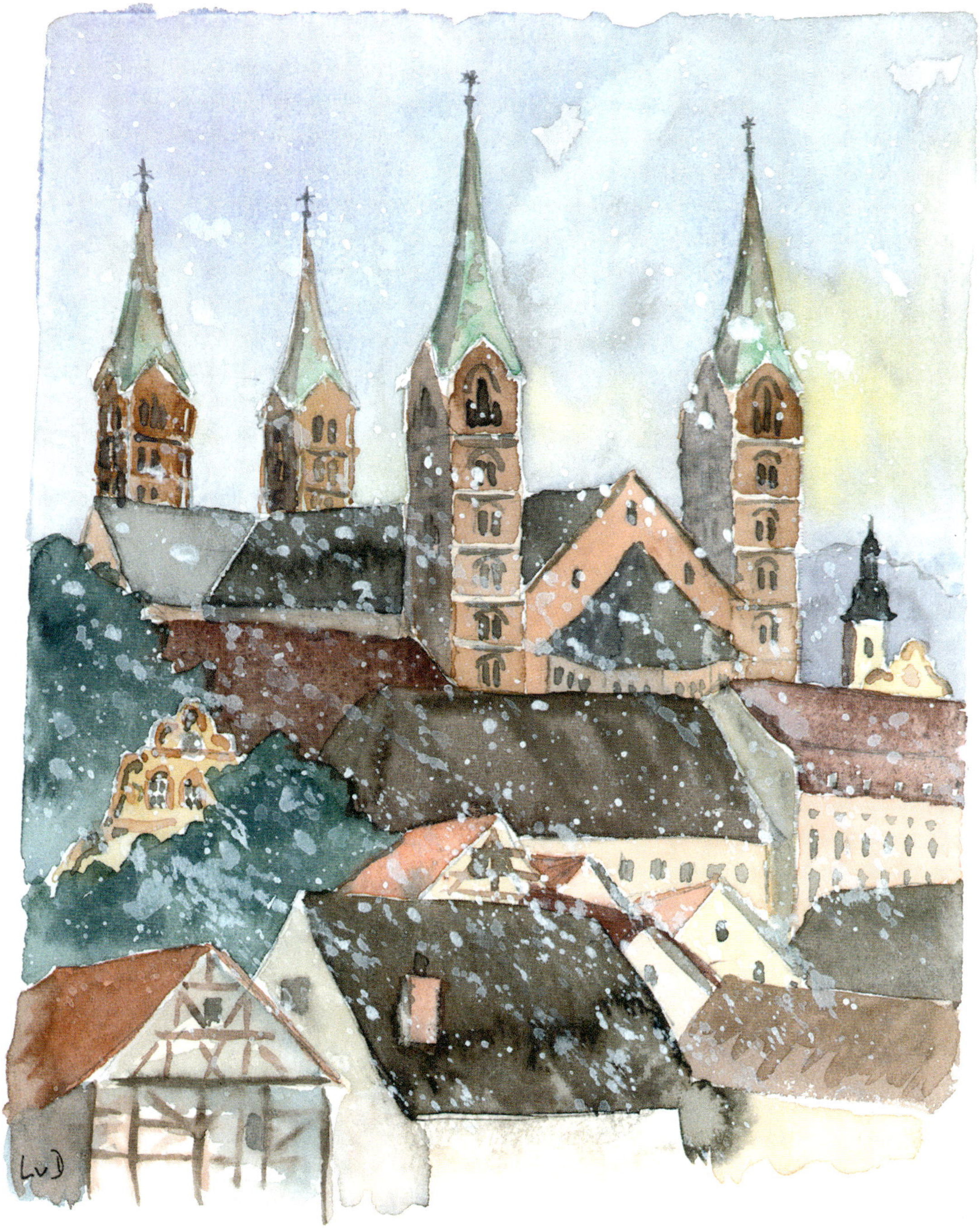
LvD

On hearing Turina's 2nd Piano Trio

These are the sounds of siesta
In the south
When oranges hang heavy on the bough
And no wind stirs the leaves.
The languid sweetness of a jasmine bloom
Behind a wall
Pervades the air,
The vast cathedral basks in a haze
Of golden light,
While in the river park
The shade is sought.
The bullring's symmetry
Shimmers in silent expectation.
And now we hear the buzzing of a bee,
The tinkling of a tiny waterfall
High in the hills
Where cattle cluster by a clump of trees.
The evening shadows lengthen,
And in the dances,
Vibrant and passionate,
Rises a sense of sorrow,
A long-forgotten grief,
That seems to emanate
From deep within
The sun-scorched earth.

Fürth, July 28th 2008
(after hearing a concert in Erlangen given by the piano trio "Triorität")

The Spider

We stopped to watch her
Spin her silken web,
A masterpiece of
Circular design.
Round and round
She trudged
In tireless toil
Until at last
The circle narrowed
To a tiny point.
Here at the hub,
Her aching legs withdrawn,
She rested,
Disguised as dusty speck,
And waited for the first
Fresh, juicy fly.

She waited
And she waited,
Frozen in seeming nonchalance,
But with her senses heightened
For that first small quiver of
thread.
It never came:
The sun went down
Upon the balcony
And on the spider's plan:
I swung the watering-can
Across the gasping flowers,
And in one inadvertent moment
I foolishly forgot
The spider's web.

Written in a café in Langenzenn
July 18th 2006

Riad Si Said, Marrakesh

The airtight plane disgorges us
Into the African night,
The russet city walls
Rise up, majestic,
To embrace us
In their maze of throbbing life.
Down narrow alleyways
Where hooded figures glide,
Past sleeping cats
And walls of hanging rugs,
Then through a vast black door
Into the pages of a fairytale:
Palm trees in a patio
With pillars, richly carved,
Rose petals floating
In a fountain's pool,
Flickering candles,
The amber glow of lamps,
A log fire casting shadows
In a niche of sumptuous cushions,
Where Aziz' friendly smile
And drinks of minted lime await us.
No sound in this oasis
Of tranquillity
Except the tinkling tune of water
As it stirs the fragrant petals,
Thus evoking
Times long past.

Nuremberg
December 8th 2008

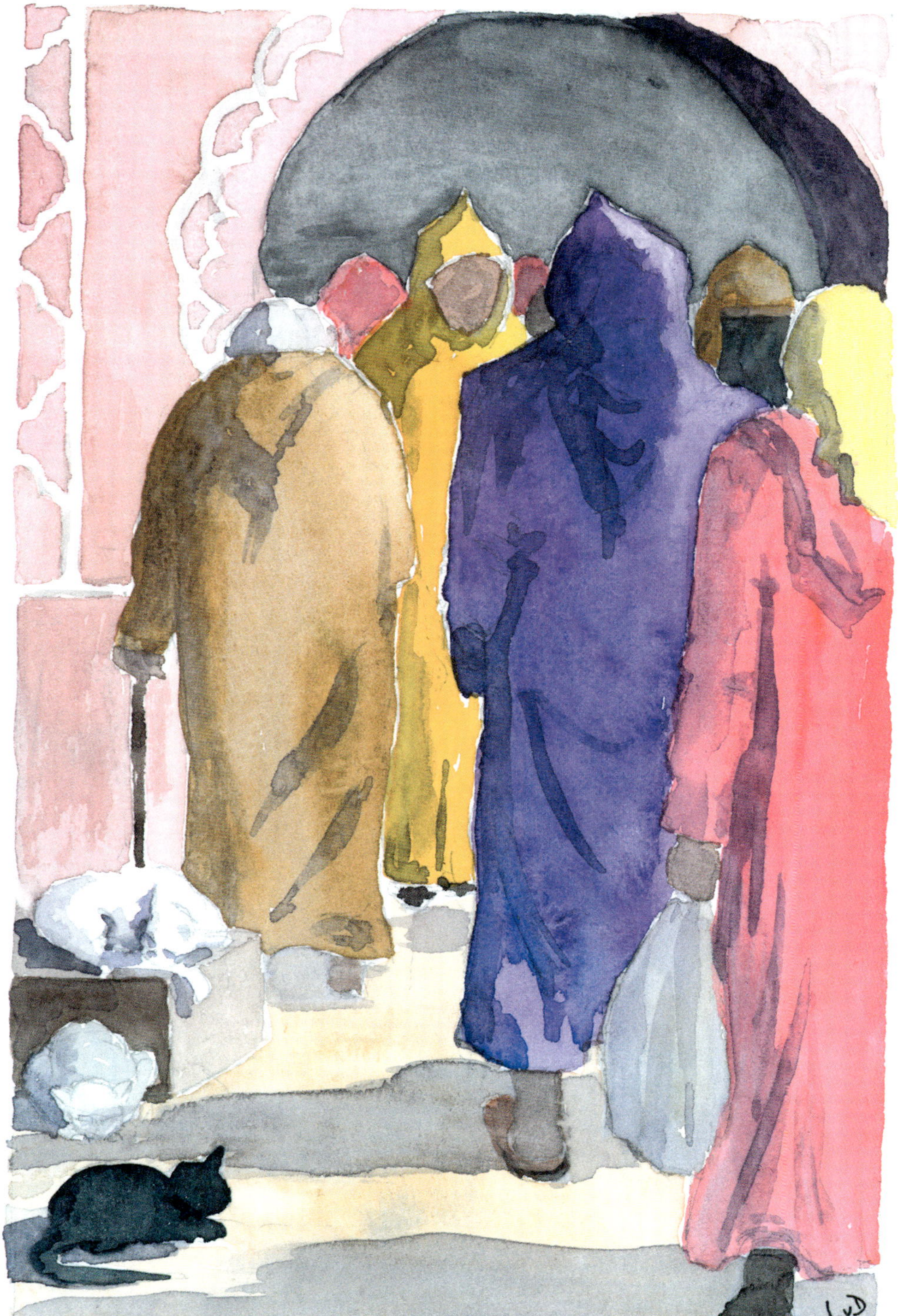
LvD

December Day in Murnau

In spite of azure skies
And dazzling snow,
Crispness of air and
Crunch of boot,
There is a brooding quality
About the mountain range
That looms above the town.
It speaks of landscape's constancy
And of our own short span.
Gone are the artists
From this lovely spot;
Gone, too, so many loved ones
From our lives.
One painting, "Park in Spring",
Captures this wistfulness
Of humankind:
A couple, slightly bent,
Has paused beneath
The blossomed crowns of cherry;
They signify the certainty of death
Regardless of new springs.

Written in the train between Murnau and Nürnberg
December 27th 2001

On Leaving the Lakes

Huddled between the luggage and the crowds
I bid my mute farewell.
The train now plunges headlong
Through the night
Unconscious of its cargo's wail of grief,
The shriek of shock at birth.
I mourn the stillness of the lake,
The rough stones underfoot,
I see again the skylark's sudden flight
From brackened hill,
The duck's head gleaming green;
And when the train
Has spewed its human freight
Into the London night,
I feel engulfed in ghastliness
And totally bereft.

London
October 14th 1996

Bagpipes in Bethlehem
(The Crib in St Michael's, Bamberg)

Greyness had blurred
The outline of the spires
And draped the town
In dampness.
All the more welcoming it was
To step into St Michael's
With its cribs and candles
And its Christmas trees.
The "heavenly garden" overhead
Arched in abundant loveliness
Above the empty nave,
While down below
The minute figures
Acted out their drama:
The patient, plodding donkey
With his precious load,
The shepherds tending to
Their restless sheep.
And, as an extra touch,
A tiny bagpipe player,
Blowing his heart out
By a flickering fire.

Written in the train from Bamberg to Fürth
January 20th 2006

Leaving Valencia

Locked in an airtight tube
We watch the twinkling toytown on the coast
Fade to a yellow blur.
We peel the airtight packaging
From tasteless roll,
Knowing that far below
Paellas sizzle in their giant pans
As countless corks are drawn.
And now you too have joined the throng
On lamplit marble pavements,
Encapsulated in that lively babbling bubble.
You relish the mellow chimes
From ancient belfries,
Savour the scents that emanate from doorways,
And breathe the musky fragrance
Of a Spanish town at night.
High up above,
Locked in our airtight tube,
We drone through lashing rain
Northwards, to colder climes.

Written on the plane from Valencia to Nuremberg
November 22nd 2007

December Swans

The swans returned at Christmas
After a year of absence,
Two sailing ships
Gliding upon the dark December water.
We watched from our kitchen window
How on Christmas Day
Their number swelled to six:
A family gathering, it seemed,
For feathered festivities.
The next day
Only the pair remained,
Family friends for us by now,
Bobbing majestically
Upon the dark December water.

Fürth
December 27th 2007

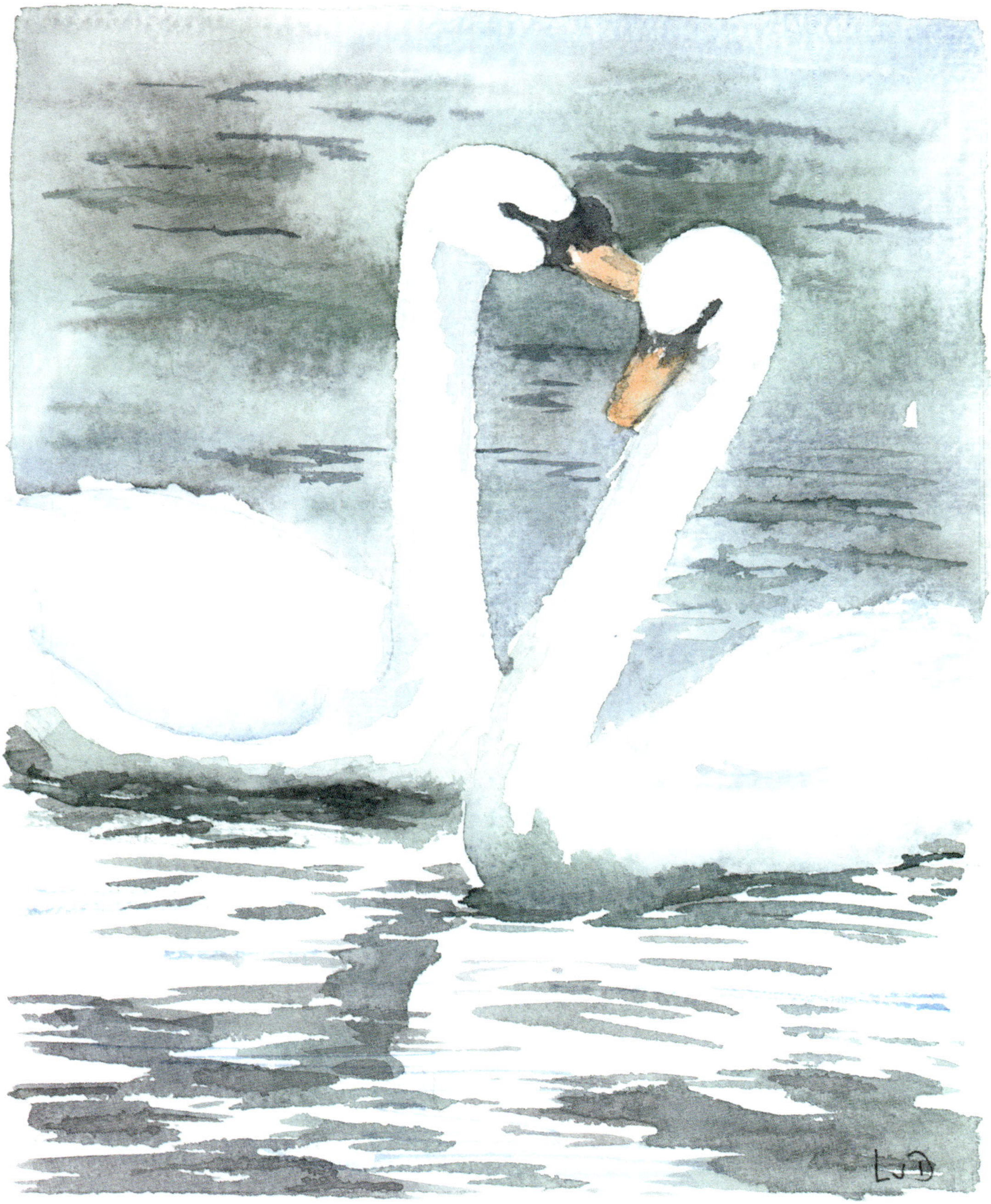

The Mount of Olives

You slept.
How could you sleep
While I confronted death
Kneeling beneath the olives
On my final night?
Shaking with fear
And loneliness
I saw you
Slouch into sleep,
Saw the tired lines
Smooth into unawareness
As reality receded.
You slept.
I felt abandoned
By you all
Yet at the same time
Overwhelmed by tenderness
And filled with a sudden surge
Of sweet sad love
For you, my closest friends.

Written in the train from Bamberg to Fürth
November 27th 2003

The Silver Canteen

I place the side knives
In their brown felt beds,
Then pause
With brandished soup spoon,
Seeing you with the sudden clarity
Of yesterday
Standing half-bent, like me,
Over the old canteen.
Contentment wars with weariness:
The dinner-party over -
But not the clearing up.
My every movement seems to mirror yours,
We share the need
To re-establish order out of chaos,
Take quiet pleasure in the
Reassuring resting place
Of each fine piece of silver.
Perhaps you gaze at me tonight,
Smiling that smile I loved
To see yourself live on in me.
Will I too gaze one day
At Steffi
As she carefully
Puts the side knives
In their brown felt beds?

Fürth
November 10th 2006

Concert in Millstatt

We step from a church of gold baroque
And ancient frescoes
Out through a glorious portal, Romanesque,
Still in a daze of pleasure.
Outside, the crescent moon,
A thin gold sickle with attendant stars,
Illuminates our path,
Easing the tough transition.
How long will those young voices
Echo in all their sweetness
In our heads?
In praise of Mary, they had soared
To the painted vaults,
Where still, no doubt, they linger.
For us, a memory already
As the present stakes its claim.
Yet we have all been touched,
Enriched, and even, imperceptibly,
Transformed:
Somewhere, deep down,
Absorbed within the very fabric of our being,
The music will continue to resound.

Millstatt
May 20th 2007

Ode to the River Mur

Fast-flowing Mur
Accompany our sleep.
Carry within the darkness of your depths
Our frailty and fears
Down to a distant sea.
Beneath the bridges
Of this ancient town
Your music pulses
In a steady roar:
Centuries of secrets
From pure mountain streams
And crashing waterfalls
Come tumbling over rocks
To wash the banks of Graz,
And will continue to,
Beyond this night
And our own tiny span.

Graz
May 17th 2003